INTENTONAL
RETENTION

SEAN BARNARD

INTENT*i*ONAL RETENTION

THE ESSENTIAL GUIDE TO HUMAN RESOURCES FOR LEADERS

Advantage | Books

Published by Advantage, Charleston, South Carolina.
Member of Advantage Media.

ADVANTAGE is a registered trademark, and the Advantage colophon is a trademark of Advantage Media Group, Inc.

Printed in the United States of America.

10 9 8 7 6 5 4 3 2 1

ISBN: 978-1-64225-756-4 (Paperback)
ISBN: 978-1-64225-755-7 (eBook)

LCCN: 2023903392

Cover design by David Taylor.
Interior design by Megan Elger.

This publication is designed to provide accurate and authoritative information in regard to the subject matter covered. It is sold with the understanding that the publisher is not engaged in rendering legal, accounting, or other professional services. If legal advice or other expert assistance is required, the services of a competent professional person should be sought.

Advantage Media helps busy entrepreneurs, CEOs, and leaders write and publish a book to grow their business and become the authority in their field. Advantage authors comprise an exclusive community of industry professionals, idea-makers, and thought leaders. Do you have a book idea or manuscript for consideration? We would love to hear from you at **AdvantageMedia.com**.

CONTENTS

ACKNOWLEDGMENTS

This book began at thirty thousand feet when I was traveling with Dr. Dustin Burleson on a trip to Las Vegas, where he was hosting one of his famous seminars. Traveling with us were friends, one of whom is a divorce attorney, and Burleson's wife. Along the way, we got to talking about some of the challenges they were having in the workplace. I gave them the best advice I could, which in turn created a conversation between Dustin and me about my passion for human resources and everything it covers. Dustin began to refer me to his own clients, and thankfully, that turned into a successful human resources consultancy business. Although I thought I would continue my journey speaking publicly, growing my own business, and helping others run theirs, by a twist of fate, I found myself being recruited by a client.

Today, I'm having the time of my life in my role as chief operating officer for a privately held dental group based in Charlotte, North Carolina. Trust me when I tell you, it *does* take a leap of faith to give up a healthy business and move over a thousand miles across the country to work with four partners. The truth is it was love at first sight, and I'm having the time of my life supporting the rapid growth of an amazing company that trusts me with creating a healthy culture for its team members.

The list of influencers who deserve credit for this book becoming a reality is endless, but I do give credit to Jason Hudson, Dr. S. Jack Burrow III, Dr. Samuel Burrow IV, Dr. Britney Welchel, Dr. Alex Culp, Gordy Kanofsky, Larry Hodges, Michelle Shriver, Julie Ragusa, Susan Varnes, and my parents (who provided a strict upbringing and introduced me to standards, respect, and the need to be humble). For me, each is a shining example of excellent leadership and mentorship.

I'm not even going to try to do what award recipients do onstage by attempting to name everyone else I'm grateful to have in my life. Candidly, there are just too many people to thank for how this book has managed to come together, the lessons that I've learned along the way, and the experiences I will share.

If you received a signed copy of this book, consider it
a token of my appreciation instead of an indication that
too many copies were printed!

FOREWORD

Every generation has its ups and downs, challenges, opportunities, and claims to fame. The past three generations, since the end of the Second World War, brought advancements in medicine, aeronautics, and computing technology. The three generations preceding the First World War brought unprecedented opportunities and evolution in manufacturing, radio technology, and communication.

Today, more people live longer and enjoy a higher standard of living than at any other point in history. Unfortunately, only a small minority of the world's population enjoy these benefits. Capitalism, free enterprise, investors, and business leaders still have a long way to go in pursuit of growth and progress.

One of the most significant achievements in modern history is the unprecedented expansion of information, knowledge, and understanding of our physical world and our place in it. From the Stone Age to the Information Age and everything in between, the magnitude of our amassed knowledge is almost incomprehensible.

When we think back to ancient Rome and the foundation for Western civilizations or the Age of Discovery and global spread of ideas, from the Renaissance to the Industrial Revolution and even the Cold War to the early Information Age, it boggles the mind to ascertain the level of detail into which our knowledge has reached in a relatively short amount of time.

In my own specialty of dentistry, orthodontics, and the treatment of cleft palate patients, the information and technology we have at our disposal today makes prior knowledge and treatment techniques obsolete faster and faster with each graduating class. A mere forty years ago, orthodontists spent inordinate amounts of time manually fabricating bands, wires, and appliances to straighten teeth. They used metal solder and pliers, heat and fire to create modern devices of their era in order to mold and shape teeth and jaws into better alignment.

Today, we use invisible beams of energy to construct 3D replicas of the patient's hard and soft tissues so that we can design and predict treatment in advance, delivered via custom braces bonded to the patient's dental enamel or via clear polyurethane trays. It would almost be impossible for the most advanced orthodontist in the world from one hundred years ago to understand even the first page of an article in today's literature about 3D printing, temporary anchorage devices, sleep apnea, airway orthodontics, biomechanics, and the science of dental materials.

And the same is true in every profession, industry, and market. We have a near-limitless amount of information available to us in all disciplines. At the click of a button or swipe of the finger, your computer or smartphone can find the answer to almost any question or curiosity.

There's a brilliant *New Yorker* cartoon that imagines what a dinner party might be like without smartphones. Someone asks, "Who was the drummer for Styx?" Around the table, each person gives an incorrect answer. The last person at the end of the table shouts with anxiety as he pulls at his hair: "OH MY GOD! We may NEVER know!"

The cartoon is funny because we've all had a similar experience at a dinner party where someone asks a question and, before they can finish speaking, the answer has been provided via smartphone inquiry. What used to take sustained curiosity and a trip to the library is today effortlessly waiting for you on the internet.

And yet, despite all this information and knowledge, decision-making has not been made easier.

Technology has made opening a business and providing products and services ten times easier, but it has not made businesses ten times better. Businesses are not ten times more profitable, ten times more equitable, diverse, or inclusive than they were six generations ago. Technology doesn't automatically create ten times the positive impact for stakeholders and the environment. Businesses aren't more meaningful to employees just because technology has made it easier to find and hire new workers.

In your career and professional niche, you've probably studied for years the latest and greatest techniques to produce excellent work and outcomes for your customers, clients, patients, or donors. While I create straight teeth and beautiful smiles, you might provide better healthcare outcomes for patients, legal resolutions for clients, products and services for consumers, or more revenue and profit for businesses and their shareholders. Regardless of your niche or industry, this constant and unending march toward more and more specialization—the acquisition of more and more technical skill—has allowed us to operate with alarmingly shallow understanding of the basics that drive results in our businesses and in our lives.

This brilliant book by Sean Barnard aims to help you in a meaningful way with one of the basics. I've known and worked with Sean as a friend and mentor. He's helped countless clients of mine in the world of coaching and professional training. His innate skill, knowledge, and passion for helping you achieve better results in your business starts with a simple yet profound understanding of people and human nature.

I've shared the stage with celebrities, professional athletes, and best-selling authors. I've spoken to live audiences numbering in the thousands, authored seven best-selling books of my own, and published professional newsletters and programs for over four thousand private practice owners in thirty-five countries worldwide. In those programs, I remind listeners and readers you can do anything you want in business, but you can't do everything. You must embrace the responsibility of leadership. You must learn how to collaborate with other people, and you must do it better than the competition.

Sean Barnard's book is an indispensable tool kit and priceless resource for anyone who wants to become a better decision maker and more effective leader. As you contemplate your place in the world, similar to other great leaders throughout every era of history, and you seek to understand how your business or organization really works, you've come to the right place. Approach the knowledge in this book with the right mindset. You'll gain a perspective that will never go out of fashion.

Dustin Burleson, DDS

INTRODUCTION

If you run a small business or manage people, who taught you how to recruit, motivate, retain, coach, or lead people? I have encountered dozens of leaders and owners who wonder why turnover is so high, morale is so low, and respect is something they can only hope for at their businesses. The answer is simple. It's because nobody trained you how to lead.

We train pilots on how to fly planes safely, chefs on how to prepare our meals to perfection, and dentists on how to put braces on our teeth with precision. But we wouldn't promote a flight attendant to fly a 747, ask a server to prepare a filet mignon or a receptionist to recommend your dental treatment. Instead, we promote good people into positions of failure by making them responsible for the well-being of others.

How many companies have elected to delegate the critical role of human resources to someone who could legally be a danger to employees, the business, and themselves? Untrained and relying on guidance from friends, relatives, or the internet for answers can be vastly more expensive than having someone trained in the basics. Yes, the alternative can be expensive, but to do nothing is reckless.

Being responsible for managing or leading others isn't hard, but it does take a passion to do the right thing, a commitment to consistency, a resilience to being labeled as the enemy when the decision isn't what someone wants to hear, and a small dash of talent to talk your way through tough conversations.

We should also talk about the ever-evolving team members of today. At the risk of sounding cliché, back in the day when my grandfather, otherwise known as Pop, took his first job on the railroads, two issues were in effect. First, he had to make the effort to go and find a job, which often meant walking door to door, making his application in person with no résumé and nothing much more than his cap in hand, and being judged purely by his appearance and first impression—all to someone superior who might barely glance up from their desk. There were only three avenues to find a job: word of mouth, recommendation, and the local newspaper.

The second—and in my opinion, most profound—difference is in how interviews were conducted then versus today. Today, we factor in a sense of equality on both ends of the interview process. It is clearly apparent that today's candidates also interview the employer to see if there is a fit. They will not take a job, regardless of pay or work conditions, if they don't feel they will belong, be respected, or have a future at the company. That is a big difference!

As an employer, I use the acronym SOAR a lot. What I owe my team members is *support*, *opportunity*, *appreciation*, and *respect*. I share that in every interview and every promotion. Of course, I make it clear what I need and expect in return—but it's important that my genuine commitment to their happiness is made clear from the beginning.

Compare that to the days of Pop Barnard, who was simply grateful to get a job, would take whatever pay was offered, and would never consider asking for a review, an increase, a bonus, or any of the perks we have grown accustomed to today.

In 1920, who would have said these during an interview?

- What type of benefits does this job come with?

- Will I receive a pay increase after ninety days?

- How many weeks of vacation do I get?

Today's workforce is evolved, but more importantly, it is bold. When representing clients, I was often asked these questions:

- What can you tell me about the employer?

- Are they nice?

- Are they friendly?

- How do they show appreciation when I do a good job?

Again, compare that to a hundred years ago, when you were told what time to show up, when you could take your break (if you got one at all), and when you were finished for the day, all without so much as a thank-you or goodbye, simply a "see you tomorrow and don't be late."

Pop Barnard, who passed away in 1979, spent his whole career on the railways. "Job hopping," as we call it today, hadn't been invented in his lifetime.

This book is designed to give the small business owner, newly promoted leader, or first-time human resources leader the tools needed. It's a book based on facts, lessons learned, mistakes made, and plenty of valuable keys to success. I want you to put this book down (preferably after reading it) and feel empowered to know what to do in nearly any situation.

Leading people is the key. If you don't lead them, they will lead you to stress, loss of sleep, drinking, quitting, or all the above. Without leadership, your team will run you down—and someone will get hurt. So read the book, and become a great people leader.

CHAPTER 1

CULTURE

—————

cul·ture

/'kelCHer/

the arts and other manifestations of human intellectual achievement regarded collectively

If I leave you with nothing else as you read this book, I sincerely hope the one thing you understand is that everything, from failure to mediocrity and the success of your business revolves around the *culture* you, as a leader, create. Culture affects the happiness and stability of our team members, the satisfaction of those we serve, and the ability to hire top talent and be an employer of choice.

The proof of an unhealthy culture is in play throughout the world. It starts with poor performance and resignations from your team members, a reputation with your customers, and the failure to meet your goals. Nobody will tell you how bad your culture is. An unhealthy culture is as silent as it is deadly to your revenue and bottom line.

Passionate and *dedicated* are two words that would describe my commitment to the culture of any place I work, whether as a team member, consultant, or leader. By no means am I perfect, and I've made more than my fair share of mistakes, but that doesn't weaken my resolve to be the best version of a good leader that I can be.

Culture relies upon commitment from the top and influences a company's priorities and standards. Culture is more than what's said in a handbook, implied in core values, or articulated in a mission statement. It's how the company lives up to the commitments and promises it makes.

Culture is reliably based on your actions and reactions. Team members will soon learn what leadership considers good or great. And when there are incentives, you can expect positive actions and behaviors to be repeated. The higher the level of leadership that rewards positive performance, the greater the impact.

> *I've lived my life with an absolute belief that being kind is the most important part of how you should treat others. Put aside everything else. That simply says it all.*
>
> **—DR. S. "JACK" BURROW, DDS, MS**

Humans drive culture, and everyone on your team contributes to either a positive or negative culture. Whichever culture is practiced most becomes engrained and, inevitably, tough to change. If the majority of your team members are positive, the negative ones will stick out like sore thumbs and often weed themselves out. This should be perceived as positive attrition.

Conversely, if the majority are negative, you are faced with an uphill challenge to turn the tide and commit every day to change. Without expecting anything to change overnight, you—as captain—can turn the ship around and recruit your officers to either get aboard or abandon it.

Culture is predicated on how you act and react and whether you talk the talk *and* walk the walk. Say anything untrue, sarcastic, demeaning, or superior, and you're off to a flying start of creating a world where nobody wants to work and where customers will sense you don't deserve their business. Nobody wants to go to a favorite hair or nail salon, restaurant, dentist, or small local store and see a fresh face every time they visit.

A positive and healthy culture is a secret weapon you must be willing to wield, hone, and maintain. This is how you will find smiling faces, devoted team members willing to share their professional hopes and dreams, and an excited team who tell friends, family, and your guests how wonderful you are to work for. The value add lies in the fact that team members won't leave you for greener pastures and an extra couple of bucks if they feel genuinely appreciated, respected, and valued. Simply put—they are happy. Best of all, you will be too.

Give your team members the tools they need to be successful. If you say you have an open-door policy, make sure you have one. Promises of any kind must be kept. Open doors for everyone to help them meet their true potential, and praise people both publicly and privately.

A healthy culture also comes with the art of coaching team members who may have strayed from your policies, procedures, handbook, or core values. Can you make that same team member feel like a million dollars despite the coaching? Can you reinforce your confidence in their future and build them up to a point where they hold a positive attitude when they leave the office? Will they walk into the breakroom and talk about the dreadful meeting they just had with you or keep it to themselves and be geared up to be the best version of themselves?

A word of caution for when you feel angry, upset, disappointed, or disillusioned by a team member: allowing your emotions to show is fruitless—and you will not be heard. Your face says everything; your words matter very little. Share your disappointment with compassion and respect, remembering to use your skills to assume positive intent. Do not corner your team member with threats or accusatory language. Instead, allow them an exit door that makes way for graceful collaboration and common ground. Ask questions with options. Here's an example.

> "Jenny, I must share that I'm disappointed with your recent performance, but I want you to give me some feedback on what might have changed from your perspective. Is there anything work related that has you 'off track'? Are you unhappy? Or is it something personal that I don't need to know about but could help shed light on your performance? We must get back to the Jenny I know."

By asking the question this way, you have established your position and the need for positive change but provided exit doors for the why and reinforced your faith in your team member as a valuable player you want to keep on your team.

Allowing your emotions to show is fruitless—and you will not be heard.

Another tip for a healthy culture is to build a reward system that targets the business goals you're aiming to reach. A quarterly bonus that recognizes loyalty is an example. An unexpected gift, such as a gas gift card, spa day, or ice cream delivery are others. A heartfelt note sent to a team member's home address, a personally written holiday greetings card, an early finish to the day, or ordering pizza for lunch and enjoying it with your team. You decide what works, and then—regardless of how much/what you can afford—make it as personal as possible.

The majority, but not all, of your team members will have professional goals. After discovering what everyone is working for and toward, build your culture chess board. As you take a mental picture of where everyone is, start the process of determining what happens "if." If Mary wins the lottery, or John is offered a salary you can't possibly compete with, or Jenny relocates out of state, or you promote Mark. What do you do? Everyone who is left behind needs to have been trained "in case." Who could be the supervisor, manager, director, or C-suite executive if someone leaves? Is anyone trained to be ready to fill those shoes? I always have my backup plan—just in case. Because life happens, and as I'll share later in this book, these wonderful people who work for you are not family. They have lives that will change course, and you need to be prepared for that.

I am passionate about the profound need for us to change our language. Not to be "woke" or keep up with the times but just because it's the right thing to do. I cringe when I hear someone referred to as *boss, management, a higher-up,* or *corporate.* I've been all those people by title or profession, but the truth is I'm worthless unless I'm a leader. Refer to yourself as a leader, because that's not just what you are; it's what you have an obligation to be and what you must be.

Remove those words from your handbooks, policies, procedures, and any signs pinned to the walls within your company. More words that are almost medieval and, to me, inappropriate for the twenty-first century? *Discipline, write-ups, warnings*, and *fired*. Call it semantics all you wish, but words are important. Although we cannot discipline, write up, or warn our team members for using these words, we can and must coach them for success. Most commonly, though, I want to see us use the words "team member." The word "employee" isn't as terrible as some alternatives that I hate. But I think team member is not just kinder, but it's also a truer description for someone who is contributing to your mutual successes.

An absolute must? The additional need to avoid the words *goal, aim*, and *aspire*. By using those words, you're implying that you haven't yet been able to meet that goal and continue to aim and aspire to being what your customers, clients, patients, and guests desire. Be bold and realistic. State the facts: "We will" at the beginning of your values, or "Our team is committed to" send an immediate message that you are committed to whatever comes next in the individual value.

From how you recruit a new team member to how you separate anyone from the company, your culture is present, at work and highly visible.

Using a reliable search engine such as Google will reveal a treasure trove of information if you ask, "What is it like to work at *X*?" or "Employee reviews for company *Y*." Despite human nature speculating that much of the feedback might stem from disgruntled former team members, look for common complaints, and ask yourself "Is that what my team thinks of me?" and "What if they do and I don't know?"

I talk later in the book about never forgetting that you are no better than the people who turn up every day and how, like you, they are not perfect. So remember to be humble, live the dream, and be the *leader* your team members deserve you to be.

Throughout the book, I have included pages entitled "Time for Tea." With a nod to my British heritage, each serves as a reminder to slow down and reflect on the lesson learned. Use them to find inspiration, and remember them as you create and build your leadership skills, a healthy workplace culture, and aspire in your core values.

TIME FOR TEA!

My passion for leadership excellence motivated me to write this book. My goal is to provide tools to anyone who leads based on what I have found useful throughout my own successes, life experiences, and mistakes over the past forty-plus years.

CHAPTER 2

COMMUNICATION IS KEY

com·mu·ni·ca·tion
/kə,myo͞onə'kāSH(ə)n/

the successful conveying of sharing ideas and feelings

The inspiration for this chapter stems from Austrian management consultant, educator, and author Peter Drucker, who wrote one of my favorite quotes: "The most important thing in communication is hearing what isn't said."

I have worked with and for many owners, directors, and managers who insist they simply don't have time to meet with their team members or, worse, claim they have nothing to say to them.

Without understanding and maintaining communication, the likelihood of losing some of your best team members undoubtedly increases.

True leadership involves two-way communication and the ability to remain connected with the team. It starts with what I call the four Vs: *visible, vocal, vested, valued.*

Before we get into the details of what those terms mean and their relevance to strong communication, I want to share an anecdote. I have tremendous respect for a leader I worked with who recognized their own failure in communication. When discussing what could be done to make a genuine connection with the team, we talked through the hurdles. After a long list of suggestions and creative discussions focusing on how the relationship could improve, there was a blurted honesty that unveiled the truth: "I'm just not comfortable doing this. I want to get to work. Plus I wouldn't know what to say anyway."

Recognizing that this is not an isolated issue becomes clear when you realize how prevalent communication, or the lack thereof, is. Grammarly, a well-respected research company, released its "State of Business Communication: The Backbone of Business Is Broken" report, revealing the far-reaching impacts of poor workplace communication on US businesses and employees. In partnership with the Harris Poll, the study estimates up to a $1.2 trillion annual loss among businesses due to ineffective communication.[1]

"Communicating well is the one critical skill that 91 percent of 1,000 employees in a recent Interact/Harris Poll said their leaders lack."

Let that sink in for a moment: 91 percent. Where and how do you start to address this challenge? By understanding that you're not alone. According to Duncan Lambden, who wrote for Expert Market in 2022, 69 percent of managers are uncomfortable when communi-

---

1   "The State of Business Communication," Grammarly Business, accessed December 1, 2022, https://www.grammarly.com/business/business-communication-report?utm_source=PR&utm_medium=article&utm_campaign=2022-GB-Harris-Poll-Report&utm_term=cta&utm_content=download-report.

cating with their employees.[2] Further, a Gallup poll estimate showed that only 50 percent of employees know what their managers expect from them.[3]

With that information, I wondered if there was any correlation between personal relationships and the ability to openly communicate. I think there is. Martha de Lacey wrote in the *Daily Mail* that men take only 88 days to tell their partner they love them compared to a woman's languorous 134.[4] A study by the *International Journal of Intercultural Relations* revealed that 62.3 percent of women and 91.2 percent of men fail to frequently tell their partner "I love you." The data tells me that statistically, nearly all of us struggle with sharing our emotions and communicating openly, freely, and more importantly, comfortably.

> *Train people well enough so they can leave. Treat them well enough so they don't want to.*
>
> **—SIR RICHARD BRANSON**

---

2   Duncan Lambden, "The Importance of Effective Workplace Communication—Statistics for 2022," Expert Market, June 13, 2022, https://www.expertmarket.com/phone-systems/workplace-communication-statistics.

3   Heather R. Huhman, "Employees Only Meet Expectations When They Know What's Expected," *Entrepreneur*, November 16, 2015, https://www.entrepreneur.com/growing-a-business/employees-only-meet-expectations-when-they-know-whats/252734#:~:text=Employees%20who%20don't%20know,expected%20of%20them%20at%20work.

4   Martha De Lacey, "When WILL He Say 'I Love You'? Men Take 88 Days to Say Those Three Words - But Girls Make Their Man Wait a Lot Longer..." *Daily Mail*, March 7, 2013, https://www.dailymail.co.uk/femail/article-2289562/I-love-Men-88-days-say-girlfriend-women-134-days-say-boyfriend.html.

HR professionals are tasked with ensuring the existence of programs that engage and retain team members for extended periods—succession planning for career pathing, training, and development programs to support professional growth, as well as rewards/recognition programs with an extensive benefits program to promote longevity.

> Nearly all of us struggle with sharing our emotions and communicating openly, freely, and more importantly, comfortably.

There is a simple truth here. To maintain a personal, healthy relationship, we know we must communicate well. Just being present and believing that flowers on Valentine's Day for your partner and a paycheck every two weeks for your team member should communicate that your care is reckless.

If you want to be perceived as a good leader (or partner), practice the four *V*s to achieve a lasting and stronger relationship with your team members.

> *Communication is your ticket to success, if you pay attention and learn to do it effectively.*
>
> **—THEO GOLD**

Start by being **visible**. People want to see you. Having you in and around the workplace demonstrates more than the fact that you, too, turned up for work today. Leaders who are visible reassure team members that there is stability. A warm smile reassures everyone that, from "the top," life is good and there's nothing to worry about. Eye contact establishes an acknowledgment that you recognize that your team members are present. One critical error, however, is visiting only some of your team members or those you work with the most. Flip the coin and spend more time being visible with those you don't interact with during the day. If your business has multiple locations, block out a week on your calendar similar to the way you would if you were on vacation or traveling overseas. Show yourself as unavailable. Instead, go on a "road show," and meet with your teams during lunch (which you should pay for and which will win you popularity, for sure).

Being **vocal** does not require you to be verbose. The need for small talk is a myth and, to the contrary, will make your audience uncomfortable. By simply ensuring that your tone of voice is upbeat and positive, even a genuine "Good morning" is often more than enough. The same applies at the end of the day when you say "Good night—thank you!" Speaking first and clearly and making eye contact with your team members allows them to respond and, hopefully, if they have something on their mind, share or ask questions. There's one extra step with this that you cannot ignore. It's critical that you listen very carefully to how your team reacts to your greeting or farewell. Remember the quote from Peter Drucker: "The most important thing in communication is hearing what isn't said."

Listen for anyone who doesn't respond or does so in anything but a similarly genuine or upbeat tone. Use those cues as alarm bells for something that you should know. All is not well—and it's up to you to find out why.

Be truly **vested** in all your team members. I saw firsthand how alarmed a team member was when the owner walked into the breakroom, stared at a cake lit up with candles, and cluelessly asked "Is it someone's birthday today?" Similarly, a joyful greeting for a team member who has just euthanized their dog is a blunder you won't easily recover from. Staying vested in and in touch with your team members means making sure you keep a list of birthdays and work anniversary dates. Maintain dialogue with everyone who shares news of a birth, death, or even a divorce with you. That doesn't mean you should acknowledge a divorce, but it does mean that you should be aware if one of your team members is simply not their usual cheerful self.

Sharing that your team is **valued** is easier than you might think. Small gestures of appreciation and acknowledgment are easy. As a brutally cold winter descended on Kansas City in 2013, I purchased a large bottle of multivitamins for our forty-plus team members and added a tag that read "Our Team Members are our #1 Asset. Stay healthy." I delivered the multivitamins personally and gave fist bumps along the way. My goal was to share that I valued them and cared about their well-being. As leaders, we can deliver a significantly more impactful sentiment by sending personal thank-you cards. They represent a more sincere message than a gift card or insignificant cash reward.

Commit yourself to having a huddle or meeting with your team a minimum of once every ninety days and update them, as much as you are comfortable, on the health, status, and future of the business. Share the good and the bad, being aware they truly want to know. Give shout-outs for new social media reviews, updates on any increase in the number of people your business has served, and ideas you've put in place from team members.

Finally, take a deep breath and say the workplace-equivalent phrase for *I love you*: "Thank you. I really do hope you all know that I appreciate and value each of you and the contributions you make to our success." It's a little longer than just "I love you," but it's not like you're saying it every day.

Another vitally important attribute along the road to wisdom in interpersonal success is to listen well. This means that you pay total attention to those that are speaking to you and not barging into the conversation because you want to insert your opinion.

—CATHERINE PULSIFER

CHAPTER 3

STANDARDS

stand·ard
/ˈstandərd/
a level of quality or attainment

> *If you are going to do something, strive to do it better than anyone else. Do it all the way. If you are going to half-ass it, why bother?*
>
> **—ASHLY LORENZANA**

I do not know that there has ever been a company that should expect to be, will be, or can be successful without a guiding light of standards. Without them, quite simply, what is the point? Without standards, you cannot expect your team members to ever do the right thing, predict what is expected of them, deliver excellence, go the extra mile, or even meet the most basic of expectations.

Standards should not be confused with rules, policies, or procedures. They are none of those. A rule can be broken when there are shades of gray and the decision is open to interpretation or conflict. Policies change depending on the needs of the business and its customers, the economic climate, politics, or myriad different reasons that make it necessary for updates and a different direction. The same can be said for procedures. These can change on a constant basis when new and improved ways of doing business are found. Standards, however, once established, should never be changed or compromised for any reason. That's why they require a great deal of thought before they are developed and published for everyone to read, understand, and live by.

Your core values should speak precisely to your standards. Do not make them flexible or open to interpretation. (We will touch on core values in another chapter.) One of my favorite standards has always been a zero tolerance for chewing gum on the job. In a company where I worked for over ten years, my intolerance for chewing gum was laughable to some. When I was transferred from one location to another, my new leader jokingly said to me, "I know how much you hate gum, but with over a thousand team members who've always chewed it, you're never going to change it. So don't stress yourself by even trying."

Well, I did not go out of my way to win and prove him wrong, but as the senior director of marketing for that property, I saw it as a standard I simply could not compromise on—and plainly refused to do so. I do not know that I stamped it out completely, but I will tell you that I drastically reduced the amount of open-mouthed smacking around there. It's not personal, as I quite enjoy chewing gum myself—and usually after a rare cup of coffee. But as a guest, especially in the world of hospitality, where food and beverage service is prevalent, I cannot think of anyone who enjoys being served by someone who is chomping gum like there is no tomorrow.

I never think it is right to chew gum in front of other people, but a lot of times I will come in for a meeting chewing gum and I will forget I'm chewing it. Then you do not want to swallow it because it stays in your system for seven years or something, so I have asked to throw it away. I have started to wonder if that is why I did not get certain movies.

—JENNIFER LAWRENCE

It is worth pointing out that if you have a standard, it must apply to everyone regardless of position, seniority, or location. I was once challenged by a human resources manager who claimed she saw no reason to not chew gum at her desk since she wasn't client facing. I reminded her that it wasn't just a standard that she was breaking but that any team member who came into her office *was* her customer and should be served with the same level of courtesy.

If you look for a shortcut, then you'll always find one. Build something incredible and embrace the formula to our future success. Set the standard for how you will intentionally direct your business after an immediate, emotional and unexpected transition.

—DR. CHARLIE CULP, DMD

Another true story involves my time as assistant general manager of a property in northern Mississippi. Corporate IT personnel were on location for the install and upgrade of our computer systems. When I confronted one of the team members and shared, as politely as I could, that the standard on my property did not allow for gum chewing, he begrudgingly spat it out and moved on with his day. A good example of where standards are good for some and not others revealed itself when it was interpreted that I was questioning the authority of the responsible senior corporate vice president, which led to me nearly losing my job. He took it personally and completely missed the point. To this day, I think he made a terrible error in judgment. Taking my career prospects with that company seriously, I looked my superior square in the eye and told him flat out that if anyone from corporate ever set foot again on a property I was responsible for, I would do the same thing all over again because that was my standard. I would not differentiate or discriminate based on someone's connections or seniority. More importantly, it was a standard that belonged to my team, and I would not jeopardize their standards for anyone. You might be asking yourself how it turned out, and the truth is corporate IT never had reason to visit again before I left the company. It's probably fair to say that I dodged a bullet. This story does have a funny ending, though. The same corporate senior leader who had threatened my employment turned out to be a huge ally and was instrumental in trying to get me to return to the company after I had left. That says more about him than it does me.

But enough about gum. It is only one of several idiosyncrasies that make me who I am!

> *Every individual, every business, every organization has a baseline of standard to which they conduct themselves. It is how high these standards are set that differentiates the average from the exceptional.*
>
> **—DR. BRITNEY WELCHEL, DMD, MS**

So how exactly do you start thinking about standards or what yours are? This should not be too difficult, as standards come naturally to many of us. You might start by figuring out what your pet peeves are. As a consumer, I have a list a mile long. Is it unreasonable to be irritated when you ask an employee in a clothing store if they have a shirt in your size and the response is "I don't think so," or worse, "Ask the team member standing there; I'm sure they will be able to find out for you." How are either of those answers helpful to me as a customer? To the first one, my response would be "If you do not know, shouldn't you find out?" and to the second, "I do not work here; why don't you go and ask them?" Both answers, in my mind, are equal to the stereotypical "That's not my job." Maybe the standard for every team member at that store should be "We will do anything we can to help our customers find exactly what they want and make helpful recommendations if we can't."

Standards can be simple.

- Telephones ring no more than four times before being answered.

- Every call is answered with a friendly greeting, stating your name as a team member and thanking the customer for calling.

- Say *thank you* instead of *uh-huh.*

- Say *lady* instead of *woman.*

- Say "Would you care for something to drink?" and not "Do you want something to drink?"

- Say "May I take your coat?" versus "Can I take your coat?"

- Say "Would you prefer a corner table?" versus "Is this OK?"

You get the picture.

TIME FOR TEA!

If you ever hear the words "But we never see you," listen! Never underestimate the power of power itself. Your team members respect you as their leader. You are someone they look up to. A kind word, a message or face-to-face dialogue with anyone who works for you can be so much more impactful than you might ever think.

One of the greatest lines came from the president of the best company I ever worked for, Ameristar Casinos (before it was sold to a company that had few moral values or genuine standards, in my opinion). He had a great mantra he expected us all to live by, whether we were dealing with customers or coworkers: "We are ladies and gentlemen serving ladies and gentlemen." Today, that might sound a little old fashioned and perhaps even stuffy, but to me it conveys exactly what should be expected if you operate any business where you're asking customers to spend money. Most of us would want to be treated as either a lady or a gentleman.

The best part of establishing standards is that once they become a part of your company culture, they are hard to shake, and you will find team members policing themselves and realizing a sense of pride in their workplace. Unlike policies and procedures, standards can be fun as well as service oriented. The rule of thumb is to make sure your team members understand you are committed to those standards and believe they're the right thing to do. I have a passion to the simple courtesies in life, especially at work. Is it so hard to open a door for somebody walking behind you or coming toward you? Is it so hard to always say please and thank you?

Look around the next time you walk into your office, store, warehouse, or wherever it is that you are the responsible leader. Look with an open eye and mind and you will see, unless you have already established standards and the most perfect workforce, where there are opportunities to set new standards or improve communication of what is important to you. Maybe, like me, you'll see opportunities in burned-out light bulbs, overflowing trash, Post-it notes stuck to computer screens in full view of customers or guests, scuffed walls, dirty carpeting, wrinkled uniforms, missing name tags, handwritten "Out of Order" notices, unpolished shoes, outdated marketing signage … and the list goes on.

A former client of mine, who I have a great working relationship with and who allows me to give her candid feedback to be the best orthodontist, found it amusing that I would challenge her about the toilet paper in her restrooms. Now, you must understand that we have an exceptionally good relationship, and I can tease her with a good heart, knowing that she understands my intentions are pure. To make my point, I asked her in front of several of her team members how much the average patient paid her for her professional services. The answer was quick. It is several thousands of dollars. "Why, then, would you subject a patient spending that amount of money to single-ply toilet paper"? She laughed and immediately agreed to change it, especially persuaded I think when one of her team members blurted out "It just scratches your … you know what!" I do not know that this is one of the most appropriate stories to share, but it does indicate a couple of things. Her standards with single-ply did not match the quality of her work, and it also proved that her team was confident enough in her to share their humorous viewpoint without fear of repercussion. That is a standard.

Sometimes it is easier to make tough decisions when you have a set of standards. Although it was a hard decision to separate employment from one of my team members, it was made easier by a phone call from our regional manager, who told me that one of our top performers had pulled her aside, pointed at our core values, and said with conviction, "I look at these, and I can honestly tell you she [the team member] doesn't live any one of these core values." We went to great lengths to try and save the situation and avoid the inevitable, but her standards were not ours and her values were not either. Sadly, we had to part ways.

> *Aspire to decency. Practice civility toward one another.*
> *Admire and emulate ethical behavior wherever*
> *you find it. Apply a rigid standard of morality*
> *to your lives; and if periodically you fail, as you*
> *surely will, adjust your lives, not the standards.*
>
> **—TED KOPPEL**

Let me share a few more of my favorite examples.

When I was responsible for one of the largest gaming operations in the Midwest several years ago, I shared with the gourmet restaurant manager a standard I had instituted in so many other properties throughout the years: Open your restaurant five minutes earlier and close five minutes later than the published times. He thought this would be an unusual standard for his restaurant and hesitated to increase his payroll expenses by adding ten minutes to his full crew every day. Conversely, try telling a lady who turns up five minutes early to your establishment that her watch is wrong, and I will tell you just how quickly you'll lose her as a customer. Guests who show up early are delighted that you're ready, but the real joy comes from watching a guest arrive at the door just as they think you are about to close and, instead of being turned away, they are welcomed in the way they would have been halfway through dinner service.

At another location, the executive team was perceived as obnoxiously superior, distant, and unapproachable, and it was a perception that we simply had to change. It was time to introduce a new standard. I asked our maintenance department to bring me fifty-four pieces of cut wood, ten inches long, four inches wide, and two inches thick. I asked our human resources director to introduce every new team member to the entire executive team at the beginning of their orientation. Bewildered but trusting, our directors and vice presidents were asked to stand in a circle. Every new team member would join them and have one leader and one or two fresh faces between them. In front of them was the stack of carefully arranged pieces of cut wood that formed a six-foot Jenga tower. One by one, everyone took their turn plucking a single piece of wood until the tower collapsed. Not only did this exercise break the ice, but it served as a first impression of the "suits" who represented the senior team as human beings who were perfectly capable of having fun and laughing at themselves. We took the game seriously and played to win against the new team members and each other, with us "suits" even behaving childishly when we lost. I think it went beyond setting the standard and enhancing the culture. The only standards that were a part of playing the game were to have fun, not be shy, and pick up the pieces and restack them for next week if you were the loser—that included me, of course! Immediately after, the executive team would retreat to our conference room and begin the weekly discussions around financial results; leadership updates; and the million-square-foot location with nine restaurants, a hotel, and the casino floor that, combined, was generating nearly a quarter of a billion dollars a year. I share that statistic not to boast but to emphasize that regardless of the size of your business, whether you have one team member or fifteen hundred, it is important to not take yourself too seriously as you still cling to your standards.

As with marathon runs and lengths of toilet paper, there had to be standards to measure up to.
—HARUKI MURAKAMI

> *You cannot mandate productivity; you must provide the tools to let people become their best.*
>
> **—STEVE JOBS**

To adopt this approach and accomplish more in your organization, follow the advice outlined by one of tech's most legendary visionaries.

TIME FOR TEA!

Which is your priority?

Your clients, customers, patients, guests, and team members or the profitability of your business?

Each is equal.

Take great care of your team members.

Let your team members take care of their clients.

Your clients will take care of you.

Repeat.

CHAPTER 4

CORE VALUES

core val·ue

/kôr/ /ˈvalyo͞o/

the central or most important part of a person's
principles or standards of behavior

> *Your personal core values define who you are,*
> *and a company's core values ultimately define*
> *the company's character and brand.*
>
> **—TONY HSIEH**

Core values are like eggs. They have a shelf life. They are best served
fresh and might need to be scrambled or fried. For good health, serve
them as often as your company changes over the years. Your business
is consistently changing, whether you like it or not. Your focus and

your goals change. Don't be frightened to change them up and make them relevant to today's needs.

Keeping them fresh is just as important as making sure everyone on your team appreciates how important they are to every measure of success.

There's one place to find the answer to every question you'll ever have—your core values. If they can't answer the question, you don't have the right core values.

With a preference to avoid vision and mission statements, I simply stick to a powerful set of core values that helps everyone understand what drives me and my company from the perspective of accountability. Indulge me as I share my top four worst-ever mission statements. Some may have changed since their original publication, but they are all, sadly, true!

"To be the most successful computer company in the world at delivering the best customer experience in markets we serve."
—Uninspiring words from Dell

"Sony is committed to developing a wide range of innovative products and multimedia services that challenge the way consumers access and enjoy digital entertainment. By ensuring synergy between businesses within the organization, Sony is constantly striving to create exciting new worlds of entertainment that can be experienced on a variety of different products."
—Easy to remember for their one-hundred-thousand-plus team members

"Undisputed Marketplace Leadership"

—Braggadocious and without reference to their product. It's clearly all about making money. Thank you, Hershey.

"Respect, Integrity, Communication and Excellence."

—Fantastical in light of the massive accounting and corporate fraud within Enron

On the other side, just to ensure you don't think of me as a cynic, here are my favorite top three.

"Organize the world's information and make it universally accessible and useful."

—Google

"We create happiness by providing the finest in entertainment for people of all ages, everywhere."

—Walt Disney

"To build a place where people can come to find and discover anything they might want to buy online."

—Amazon

One of the best leaders I had the privilege to work for was Larry Hodges, former president of Ameristar Casinos. He never raised his voice or was anything but a gentleman. But with grace, he would expect the highest standards, performance, and behavior from everyone. I loved having Larry as one of my most senior leaders—and he treated me well, but at the same time I was scared to death of him. Explaining what it was like to work for Larry, I share an analogy that I came to realize was also revealing of my own leadership style: "I swear he's got a baseball bat in his office. I've never seen it and never want to. But I have no doubt in my mind that he's got one."

I'm never the "boss" unless you make me one. I'm just a guy with a different title and different responsibilities. In truth, I'm your leader and responsible for what you do.

Michelle Shriver, another great leader I had the privilege of working for, taught me an incredibly valuable lesson about sharing great ideas. As the senior vice president of one of seven casino resorts, she shared how frowned upon it was for anyone to have a great idea if they kept it to themselves. Apparently, years prior, a senior leader had shared with her how he had saved the company $250,000 over the previous twelve months using a best practice with one of the seven casinos he worked at. Instead of the praise he was expecting, he was admonished for not bringing his idea to the bigger table. Think about it. He had saved $250,000 for that one casino, but the company had lost the opportunity to save an additional $1.5 million on the rest of the six. Great ideas become "best practices," and they should always be shared to maximize their value.

> *There are some values that you should never compromise on to stay true to yourself; you should be brave to stand up for what you truly believe in even if you stand alone.*
>
> **—ROY T. BENNETT**

Something that has always baffled me is how the higher up you are in a company, the more forgiving owners and senior leadership are toward your blunders in comparison to the most insignificant misdemeanors of frontline team members. How can that be? "Do we wonder why our hourly team members have no respect for us when they see some of the things we get away with?" I asked my senior team. For someone who works the front line, earns eighteen dollars an hour, and takes abuse from customers, I have an immense amount of patience and forgiveness. If they were snappy and sarcastic, or left early, came in late, or missed a day—so what? Do we hold the director of a department who's earning $200,000 a year—five times what the frontline team member is earning—to the same standards? Why not? What are we afraid of? The higher you go, the higher my standards and expectations. About five times higher.

If you want to argue, debate, or battle with me over any subject, you'll realize I live by the three *C*s: *courtesy*, *conciseness*, and *constructiveness*. Treat me with the same respect I'll show you. Don't spend an hour making your point. Keep it constructive. In return, you'll receive the three *R*s: *respect*, *rational*, and *reasoning*.

For any organization to be successful, there must be three components that are equally vital: *structure*, *process*, and *empowerment*. Without these, you can't expect your team members to act with confidence in any situation.

Team members are like CHALK and cheese. Cheerful, helpful, approachable, likable, kind are the ones I want to work with. Avoid the cheese. Eventually, it goes off.

> *A diamond is merely a lump of coal*
> *that did well under pressure.*
>
> **—HENRY KISSINGER**

Also according to Henry Kissinger, "It's more than obvious, but it's worth saying what's true: humans drive all progress. They're the ultimate resource."

Moving on from the topic of standards, core values are the perfect segue to one of my favorite subjects and passions. Chief executive officer Gordy Kanofsky; company president Larry Hodges; and my immediate leader, senior vice president and overseer of all Ameristar properties Michelle Shriver were instrumental in creating the core values for Ameristar. They didn't just help create them; they lived them through every day-to-day action and reaction. Although it went unspoken, we knew we were expected to know the core values by heart and be able to repeat them verbatim.

There were so many things I loved about our core values. For one, they applied to everyone—and I mean everyone. As a senior vice president of the company, not only was I expected to live the core values, but I also quickly realized that the people I reported to also held themselves accountable to them and lived them too. If you are not prepared to genuinely live by the core values you expect or demand from your team members, I have one piece of advice: don't bother writing them.

I recall vividly a good anecdote that occurred during a quarterly meeting at our corporate offices in Las Vegas. I will not go into detail, but suffice it to say that a change in law negatively affected all our team members, including those paid hourly. The finance vice president quickly pointed out that the net effect of the change would net the company millions of dollars a year in savings. There were slight murmurs of approval among the group of senior staff from each property as well as the corporate team that met regularly to discuss the company's financials. I watched, listened, and then witnessed firsthand the reactions of the most senior leaders—who let me add, would individually and collectively lose little. Their reaction was priceless and spoke to how they lived our core values. They made it perfectly clear to everyone

> If you are not prepared to genuinely live by the core values you expect or demand from your team members, I have one piece of advice: don't bother writing them.

in the room that nobody who worked for Ameristar would lose because of the change. Instead, anyone who might be negatively affected would receive an immediate increase in compensation that would be equal to anything they might have been shortchanged. How easy it would have been for them to enjoy instant bottom-line profit and see something taken away from people they did not work directly with. That could have been passed on to the likes of me to deliver as bad news, but instead they lived our core value: *Do the right thing, even when no one is looking.* I will never forget that. The truth is, so few people in this company made up of thousands of team members ever knew what could have happened or how passionately senior leadership felt about doing the right thing. Sadly, those who came after them did not have the same respect for their team members or an inherent goodness. At least I never witnessed it.

I have written several sets of core values over the years since leaving Ameristar, but wherever I can, I incorporate two incredibly special and meaningful components of those I hold dear. When I can't fit them in to the core values, they simply become a standard or expected best practice!

- Always do the right thing, even when no one is looking.

- Always assume positive intent.

Those close to me know I use the latter because it is a personal flaw of mine that I work on every day. My mind will frequently go to the dark side, and I have called myself out too many times for not taking good intentions into account as my instinctive first thought. As a leader, I advise you to remember that when writing your core values, add something that will make you a better leader and can support you in holding yourself more accountable. Without that, I know I would not have been as successful or happy. I take pride in knowing when I have caught myself thinking positively before succumbing to the temptation of thinking negatively.

I have guided employers and clients to give me five—and if they *need to*, one or two additional—buzzwords that either indicate their passions, standards, needs, wants, or desires for their company or business. Naturally, there are several similarities in the responses I receive. Responses like excellent customer service, communication, cleanliness, quality product, great reputation, team happiness, and fun are some of the most common.

From there, I select some words that stand out based on how well I know the business. Often, you can tell they list their true passions first, and by the time they get to number six or seven, they are stretching to make the list longer versus keeping to their desired top five.

If possible, but not necessary, make the first letter of each core value equal to an acronym that can easily be remembered. I cannot say that I did that with my own company when I created ours. *Team. Respect. Integrity. Support. Standards.* Even though I could have rearranged the order to read STIRS instead of TRISS, the team that worked on it insisted that *team* should come first.

Once you have created your core values, publish them in your client/customer/patient/guest areas and break rooms. Reward the team members who live by these core values. Shout them out as loud as you can—unless you don't truly love every word of the messaging or don't have a genuine belief in each one.

My favorite so far, other than those at Ameristar, is for a client who thankfully became my employer. Each of the four partners at their firm not only approved of the new core values when I created them, but they genuinely *lived* them. So, when it was time, we finally published them as "Our 5 STEPS to Staying Smiles Ahead." *Service, teamwork, ethics, promises,* and *standards.*

1. Service—Never forgetting the patient *always* comes first.

2. Teamwork—All for one and one for all.

3. Ethics—Simply doing what's right.

4. Promises—Once we make them, we never break them.

5. Standards—Better than yesterday, even better tomorrow.

Next, make sure that the key words are the only singular factor you insist every team member understands, remembers, and can share about without hesitation if asked. The statements that follow are just as important for writing down and sharing with your team members and your guests or customers or clients. But if anyone repeats the true intent without the exact wording, that is good enough for me.

I am happy to share the ones I wrote for my beauty salons. I'm giving you freedom to copy them, just as I (once again) drew inspiration for them to some degree from Ameristar Casinos.

1. Team—We are a fun, service oriented, and productive team.

2. Respect—We treat everyone with respect and assume positive intent, every day with everyone.

3. Integrity—We will do the right thing, even when no one is looking.

4. Support—We support a positive, responsible, and inclusive environment, internally and within our communities.

5. Standards—We promise high standards in an enjoyable, welcoming, and clean environment.

TIME FOR TEA!

Well-written core values can answer any question you have, decision you must make, or direction you must take, no matter how difficult or complex.

Think of any stressful decision you have had to make in the past ninety days where you had one of two or more options. If you are thinking about separating from one of your team members, ask yourself:

- Do they live by *our* core values?

- Have I lived by *our* core values?

Business leaders sometimes find themselves in situations where they need to decide whether to refund money to a problem customer whom they know is either taking advantage of them, trying to beat the system, or simply cheating the business out of its hard-earned money. Here is a great example of how it is easy to get sucked into the dark side and think the worst. Even if you know you are right, look to your core values. I have found over the years that those who try to cheat you usually do so only once. A good example is the customer who has simply changed their mind on a product and wants a full refund despite them having opened the bottle of perfume, worn the shirt, or broken whatever it may be they purchased. So, assume positive intent, and ask yourself, *What if I am wrong?* How would refusing a refund be the right decision, and what message does it send to your team?

When I first created my beauty salon brand, the first location I bought had a no-refund-for-any-reason policy already in place. When asked why, several of the stylists explained that consumers sometimes bought shampoo or conditioner and used it a couple of times before realizing they did not like it. Then they'd refill the bottle to the brim with water before returning it. I overturned that policy the first week of ownership for two reasons. Word gets out that you do not do refunds because you do not trust your customers. It only takes one incident in the presence of any other customer who overhears not just the policy but why the policy exists for them to realize that the owner thinks of everyone as a potential cheat or thief. That is simply bad business if only because that guest or customer and everyone who comes behind them will be reluctant to take a chance on a new, highly recommended product knowing full well that if they do not like it, they cannot return it. So, in addition to its being completely contrary to your core values—if they are the same as mine—this policy is also plain bad business practice. Instead, happily refund the purchase and apologize that it did not meet their expectations. With that simple gesture, you will have immediately hit on three of our core values: you treated the guest with respect, you did the right thing, and you delivered on the promise of an enjoyable and welcoming environment. What is the worst thing that can happen? Somebody who is cheating you tries again. You can deal with that by treating them with respect and asking them to please be sure before they purchase. What is the best thing that can happen? Retail sales and customer loyalty increase alongside team member morale because they no longer must face angry customers who are asking for an accommodation in good faith.

Let's look at another example. One of our team members who works at the front desk complained that her computer crashed at least three times a week. She was not frustrated, and she was not annoyed—she simply wanted me to know because sometimes it would cause her to delay a guest who was calling in or trying to check out. A quick look at our core values tells you exactly what decision you must make. Buy a new computer the same day, and worry about whether you can repair or repurpose the old one later. Which core values did we hit here? First, I give credit to the team member who shared the problem. She assumed positive intent by making the decision to tell me and was confident she would not be ignored or have her concerns disregarded. In addition to doing the right thing, I am providing her with the tools she needs before the situation worsens and the computer crashes. We delivered on our standards by ensuring that the experience for not just the guest but for her was pleasant whenever she logged on. I challenge anyone to give me a situation where well-written core values will not provide you with the right answer.

The last example I will share is also a true story. A team member who worked at a restaurant was notoriously and perpetually late for work and, therefore, unreliable. She was negatively affecting the morale of the team and, at the same time, our commitment to timely service for our guests. One of the many standards, or you could say policies, that I mentioned earlier insisted that no team member could be terminated or as I prefer to call it, separated, from the company without my approval unless drugs, theft, fighting or another proven zero-tolerance policy had been violated. I cannot quite remember the exact thresholds for violation, but we operated our attendance policy using a points system—

> I challenge anyone to give me a situation where well-written core values will not provide you with the right answer.

half a point for being tardy, a full point for an unapproved absence, and two points for what we termed a "no call, no show." She was fast approaching the established threshold, and her supervisor had created the paper trail that was required before the final tipping point was reached. Her file came to my desk for approval to separate her from the company. I asked the director who oversaw all our restaurants what exactly he had done to investigate why she was late for work and for how long this situation had been a problem. He did not know. First mistake. Was anyone going to assume positive intent and ask what is going on and why she was coming into work late so frequently after many years of a perfect time and attendance record? The director of human resources—whom I also held accountable for not living our core values because she failed to investigate further on the tardiness—and I called the server into my office and asked if there was something she wanted to share. Breaking down in tears, the server said that for years, she had been physically abused by her husband. Recently, he had gotten arrested for a robbery, which finally set her free but also left her with no one to watch her children before her mother came home from work so she herself could arrive on time for her work shift. I sensed we had let her down, if only because she did not trust us enough to tell us the truth or ask for help sooner. And perhaps much of it was because she was embarrassed or scared to tell us, ashamed of the life that she had been living and the husband who had not only abused her but was now a felon. Here was the catch: figuring out what to do when you are responsible for enforcing the policies of the company. The rules were clear. Exceed the number of time and attendance violations and you lose your job. Eureka. Turn to your core values. Do the right thing. We were able to refer her to a team member assistance program, but better still, we changed her schedule so that she could be on time. True, she was the only server permitted to start her shift an hour later than anyone else, but I defy anyone to tell me that living by the rules would not have been a gross violation of our core values. I did have to report this to Michelle, my leader, and it was no surprise she supported the decision 100 percent. I can almost hear the most cynical reader challenging the decision by questioning where and how you draw the line for the next team member with a problem greater or lesser. My response to that would be that I will worry about that when the time comes. Could a team member who was separated for time and attendance claim unfair dismissal because I broke the rules for one and should again? Sure. But I would defend that decision with the full knowledge that I had the support of my company and its core values behind me.

Another important point to make about your core values: Broadcast them. Talk about them. Brag about them. Post them for everyone to see in public areas and back of house. But whatever else you do—live them!

Allow me to conclude this chapter slightly off topic but related, nonetheless. I have very strong feelings about *not* having a point system in effect for team member tardiness or absence. I've outlined the reasons that support that with the story of the tardy team member. Now, I always rely upon a system that requires leaders to be alert and look for pattern absences: requests for an early finish to the day or late arrivals at the beginning of each day. A team member who is regularly too sick to come to work every Monday or feels too ill to finish work on a Friday are the patterns I'm referring to. I can hear you asking why I would choose a subjective policy versus one that is objective or measurable or defensible. It is subjective, but it is also certainly still defensible. You are living your core values (hopefully) and treating everyone as individuals anytime a pattern appears. Defensible? Well certainly you can still be attacked with a discrimination suit, but I think that if you stay on top of it and see a pattern and address each as a single issue, you build morale, and those who want to take advantage will get caught out sooner or later. Claims of "She's been out just as often as I have" fall to the wayside when you consider a lack of reliability versus a pattern. The key is to make sure your handbook is clearly written. The company reserves the right to separate from anyone who has pattern absenteeism or tardiness, negatively affecting the morale of their coworkers or customers.

> *If you give people tools, and they use their natural abilities and their curiosity, they will develop things in ways that will surprise you very much beyond what you might have expected.*

—BILL GATES

Bill Gates encompasses many of the values we should hold dear in our organizations, irrespective of size, and there is much you can learn from his powerful quotes and sayings. Set standards that are not only uncompromising but fair, enforceable, understandable, and reasonable. Ask yourself what your standards are. If you are a leader of directors, managers, or supervisors, ask them the same question—what are your standards? You will be pleased and surprised with several of the responses, but regretfully there will also be occasions where you will walk away disappointed for two reasons. The first is because they might not have any standards. The second might be that they do not know what *yours* are. A smart thinker, at the very least, regurgitates what they know their leader holds dear as a standard.

CHAPTER 5

THE ART OF RECRUITMENT

re·cruit·ment

/rəˈkro͞otmənt/

the action of finding new people to join an
organization or support a cause

This chapter wholeheartedly covers the art of recruitment. Many of you will think this as a fancy way of saying *hiring*. And it is. However, it is also an art and should be treated that way if you want to hire the *right* people. There are many who think hiring is one of the easiest tasks for frontline supervisors, leaders, and even directors.

However, let us pause for a minute and examine the flip side of the coin. Consider what it is like when you have to say goodbye to someone—the opposite of the hiring process, or so you would think.

When it is time to say goodbye to a team member, whether for a good cause or otherwise, we go to great lengths to dot our i's and cross our t's. The person charged with this insufferable task checks with the supervisor, or the leader they report to, in the hopes that they will share the burden in case a wrongful dismissal suit is filed. We check and double-check the handbook, presuming there is one, and in some cases, reach out for legal advice. For those who are in executive positions, there is much to think about: documentation, severance payouts, COBRA, and the memo that must go out to everyone explaining why John or Mary is no longer with the company. We lose sleep, we second-guess our decision, and finally (hopefully) determine that the course of action we are taking is the right one.

> *Don't hire anyone you wouldn't want to run into in the hallway at three in the morning.*
> **—TINA FEY**

So, here is the big connection. Why is it that so many with the power and authority to hire rush in blindly with no real thought or plan? My contention is that the art of recruitment is a multifaceted and complex decision-making process that should take as much, if not more, work and preparation than it takes to say goodbye to someone.

Despite millions of unemployed Americans, there continues to be a huge gap between the quality of applicants and the demands of the decision makers.

Open positions in some fields frequently exceed the number of résumés on quality employment websites. Looking for an experienced team member on Indeed, Zip Recruiter, or Monster can be frustrating to a leader and a recruiter.

Unemployment for well-educated workers is remarkably low—and has been throughout the pandemic and ever since. The same applies to mature workers. They are settled or have settled and don't want change.

Maybe you're asking why you are experiencing high turnover? Here's some insight into why you are likely losing people and how to stem the tide. FlexJobs surveyed more than two thousand people nationwide and found a variety of factors influencing people's decisions to leave their jobs.

The top reasons workers gave were a toxic company culture (62 percent), low salary (59 percent), poor management (56 percent), and a lack of work-life balance (49 percent). Work-life balance is a tough subject for many leaders as it is almost impossible for a business with set hours of operation. Can you change the turnover rate? I think it's always an uphill struggle, but one we take on by virtue of the responsibilities we accept as leaders. Recognition tops the list.

Vantage Circle reported 44 percent of employees switch jobs because of not getting adequate recognition for their efforts.[5] In 2022, CNBC shared a surprising statistic, with 25 percent of employees reportedly citing a "toxic company culture."[6] If you aggressively commit to making changes and addressing issues important to your team members, you can realistically move the bar. Start today.

---

5   Vantage Circle, "25 Employee Recognition Statistics You Shouldn't Ignore in 2022," blog.vantagecircle.com, updated September 5, 2022, https://blog.vantagecircle.com/employee-recognition-statistics/.

6   Kate Dare, "Toxic company culture is the No. 1 reason workers are quitting jobs, survey finds," CNBC, April 13, 2022, https://www.cnbc.com/2022/04/13/toxic-company-culture-is-the-no-1-reason-workers-are-quitting-jobs.html.

TIME FOR TEA!

Go into every interview with the tools you need: experience minimums, qualifications, education, salary range, job description, etc. But not before determining what your perfect candidate avatar is and a belief that personal skills, which are embedded in everyone's DNA, are always considerably more valuable than technical abilities.

When employers are ready to hire, they make a list of attributes to include in the job posting. Of course, *experienced* is at the top of that list. Then follows a list of skills that qualify who would be a perfect fit for the role. It's not unusual for an owner or executive to say "Find me someone disciplined, adaptable and able to work both independently and as part of a team."

Employers frequently become frustrated when the ideal new hire doesn't complete their onboarding period. How could this be? With years of experience and having passed both background and reference checks, what went wrong?

Don't hesitate in how you promote the opportunity—but be clear. Advertising jobs that might be unsuitable for a candidate, and lack clarity of expectations is not only wasting time but also unfair to everyone involved: candidate, recruiter, and the leader. It's time to think outside of the box.

Today, there are just too many hiring managers who lack the skills and basic abilities to make a good decision. Why? Simply said, they were never trained correctly (or at all), or they just did not give the hiring process the thought that it deserves. Often, these hiring managers are provided with nothing more than a salary range, a job description, and a title. Does anyone really sit down anymore and ask themselves what they are looking for (precisely) in a qualified candidate? Typically, we know why the last person failed, but do we really know what will make the next person succeed? Do we consider how much of the fault of failure lies with the previous team member versus with us?

> Today, there are just too many hiring managers who lack the skills and basic abilities to make a good decision.

Let's start with the job description. We must ask certain questions before we even consider interviewing:

- **Is the job description current and realistic?**

  When a team member holds a job for a long time, it is pretty much a given that their job description will have changed over time. Duties change and/or shift to others on the team. While leadership, managers, and HR should write the job description, the team must come together to understand the true personality traits and skills needed for any candidate to succeed at the position. You should be generating a concise and accurate description including, but not limited to, an appropriate title, duties performed, skills required, personality traits desired, and salary range. Add any job-related duties that might be a hazard to candidates, such as climbing, being exposed to chemicals, standing for long periods of time, etc. And share each of those potential risks during the interview process, not once the candidate is onboarding and others have been rejected. By ensuring that the job description is current, you are ensuring that the right people apply and that you are contributing to a positive company culture. Sharing a job description with any candidate—externally or internally—is smart. Why wouldn't you? Nothing to hide and everything to gain.

- **Is the salary range competitive to salaries of other team members who perform a similar job function? Does the compensation package contain everything that you need it to?**

  One of the easiest quagmires to walk into is arbitrarily realizing that the market demands you pay a higher rate for a position. The problems with that are obvious. Who else holds a similar position now that will then earn less? Or even worse, which protected classes will be left behind? Is there a cap on the wage or salary? Without it, and with annual increases, it is not impossible for a candidate to believe they are due a 5 percent increase. Think about a team member who starts at fifteen dollars an hour and remains in the same position for twenty years. Is that same position now worth over forty dollars per hour? This is the same person who's performed well for you, has perfect attendance, a great attitude, and gets perfect reviews each year, but at the same time, the same number of widgets are being put into the same number of boxes. Develop your entry-level pay range and the most you would be willing to compensate, knowing that the market may dictate changes later. By creating a low-mid-high range for every position, you create a structure that allows you to make the right decisions. When someone hits the high range and is capped, it's wise to consider a lump sum payout as a reward for an additional year of service, but with one caveat. Ask yourself, did the team member *earn* the payout, and can you justify it? Or are you just trying to keep the peace and rewarding them for another year under their belt? It's not difficult to figure out which of the two is the right answer.

- **Who will this person report to, and what are their idiosyncrasies, likes, and dislikes?**

  You cannot discriminate by preferring to hire younger versus older, taller versus shorter, Republican or Democrat … and the list goes on. But you can have an objective preference for a team member who is highly focused on their work and remarkably accurate. In some states, you might not be able to discriminate against hairstyles, but you can demand the candidate flawlessly execute a customer service issue.

> *Aim for success, not perfection. Never give up your right to be wrong, because then you will lose the ability to learn new things and move forward with your life.*
>
> **—UNKNOWN**

Where and how you advertise for the position is also important. Quite obviously, you would not post for an executive chef position on Craigslist any more than you would list an open position for a dishwasher on Indeed or Monster Jobs. Defining where best to advertise is a wise step many fail to consider, which leads to recklessly spending company money on a jobsite just because "that's where we always advertise."

The next consideration is this: What does the job posting look like, and how well will it read and capture the attention of your ideal candidate? If you take the time to view other postings, you will see some atrocious writing, very much telling about the posting company and its lack of attention to detail. The header alone is integral and should be made to stand out from every other position, no matter how similar they may be to yours. One of my favorites was a posting I placed several years ago for a customer service call center job. It simply said, "Can you answer a telephone?" It may seem juvenile or even patronizing, but the click-through rate for applicants who opened and read the posting itself helped us fill the position in days rather than weeks, consequently saving us a lot of money. Filling positions quickly with the right candidate saves time because you're not left having to respond to hordes of unqualified candidates you'd otherwise attract and who would still be entitled to a response, regardless of their unsuitability.

Another easy trap to fall into is making the job sound so fantastic that it seems too good to be true—because it is. I frequently tell candidates when I interview them, especially for leadership and executive positions, that I am going to make every effort to talk them *out* of the job. Although you do not want to do that in a job posting, *it is critical that you keep it realistic*. Whether the hours are long, there is a great deal of standing, you cannot guarantee the number of hours per week for a part-time position, or the position consists of mindless work, you need to figure out how to say whatever needs to be said so you don't waste time interviewing people who have an unrealistic expectation of the job. The added bonus of creating the perfect posting is the reduction in the number of applications you will have to parse. To illustrate this, if you are hiring for a qualified dental assistant and many of your applicants' most recent positions are with fast food restaurants, it is likely that your posting was not clear enough.

I also want to add that many leaders who post positions know that their coworkers, team members, and leadership will see that position and may question their messaging. To them, I would simply say this: I need to find the right person who understands exactly what this job is about, what is expected of them, and how they will be successful. My job is not to sell the position; it is to hire for the position.

To me, plowing through applications and résumés is what I expect online dating to be like—except without the pictures. You have the unenviable task of trying to create an image of the person applying for the job simply by going off their work experience, education, and the usual blurb about their objectives and why they're the ideal candidate, knowing fully well that they put the same information on every résumé. Your job is to sort through the haystack and find the few needles you want to interview. Let me just say right off the bat that some of the best candidates I have ever interviewed have had the worst résumés. This is a great time to mention the need to assume positive intent. Not everyone is an expert résumé writer. And some even have a friend, a relative, or a third party write it. Get past it. Look for the beef and what *you* want.

So how do you figure out who to invite to the next step in the interview process? That often comes down to your gut feelings and ability to read past the fluff to look for the qualifications you need, because at the end of the day there is not much else you have to go on. I personally do not like wasting my time interviewing people any more than the next person, and I have no hesitation in cutting an interview short with good grace and manners if it is clear that the applicant and I are wasting each other's time. My preference for an interview is always face to face, either in person or virtually where I can see and learn so much about who exactly I'm interviewing. In the age of Zoom and Google, there have, quite frankly, been some horrendous and, at times, hysterical interviews that I have conducted. Faces too close to the screen, people sitting in darkness, candidates using their phones and wandering around their apartments are not uncommon. One of the most frustrating things to me is that over half the people I interview waste a couple of minutes trying to connect and then joyfully and, without excuse or apology, announce "This is my first time using Zoom." How could you possibly be so unprepared for a job that pays $50,000 a year or more?

Aim for success, not perfection. Never give up your right to be wrong, because then you will lose the ability to learn new things and move forward with your life.

—UNKNOWN

Here are three of my all-time favorite interview stories:

Candidate #1 was interviewing for a highly paid office manager position. She sat on the floor of her living room in front of her couch and stroked the belly of her dog constantly throughout the interview.

Candidate #2 was fifteen minutes late for her interview, and when nudged by me via text to see if she was still interested, she responded yes. When we talked, it was evident she was in a drugstore picking up some groceries.

Candidate #3, however, is the clear winner. After logging in late and having to be told that her camera was pointed at her laundry hamper and open bedroom closet, she turned the camera to herself, which clearly showed she was still in bed.

So, therefore, I say that looking at résumés and applications and interviewing is like online dating. Meeting your top five or six candidates must be the closest thing there is to a speed dating session. The candidate is nervous and, most likely to a degree, so are you. You have limited time to get to know this person and ask him or her all the relevant questions and, just like dating, figure out if they're someone you want to be with or would recommend to your direct supervisor or a coworker.

To offset some of this anxiety, I avoid asking the typical questions many candidates expect to be asked. I really think it is almost insulting when the standard questions start to roll out, such as "Where do you expect to be in five years?" or "Tell me about a situation that made you uncomfortable, and how you resolved it." Or "What are your hobbies?" or "Why did you apply for this job?" If I interviewed for a job and somebody asked me those questions, I would be so tempted to answer those questions respectively with "Sitting behind your desk" and "I told them I didn't care" and "Skydiving" and "Because I'm unemployed." Yet to this day, that is the set of questions many good candidates are asked, and it is a complete waste of your time and theirs. Why not simply ask them what you really want to know? Again, just like speed dating, wouldn't you want to know the truth?

Here are some of my favorite interview questions. Each has revealed so much about the person:

- What drives you absolutely crazy at work to the point where you want to go home and scream?

- Describe your sense of humor.

- What will make you go home within ninety days and start looking for another job?

- If I were to ask you for an example of when you could not have been prouder of yourself at work, what would you say?

- If you had to guess, what one skill, personality trait, or habit would I ask you to improve upon when you receive your first review?

You will be surprised by the answers that you get. During a telephone interview several years ago, a candidate who was clearly qualified for a position and had a remarkably strong résumé and references spoke in a monotone that almost sounded like he was about to flatline. It was then that I asked him about his sense of humor. He paused, and then blurted out laughing as he said it: "Goofy!" For whatever reason, it broke the ice, and we had a good interview. And yes, he got the job. Ask questions the candidate has not heard before—not to catch them off guard, show them how clever you are, or embarrass them, but to find out who they really are. You will find it extremely rewarding. You will also find that the interviewee appreciates the change of pace and questions and enjoys the interview, whether they get the job or not.

A former vice president who worked for me at a casino had one of the smartest ideas about how and when to interview, which, together, we took a stage further. She was hiring for a position that would work from 8:00 p.m. until 4:00 a.m. and where customers were allowed to smoke. She decided that the best time to interview them was 1:00 a.m., in the early hours of Sunday morning, standing in the center of the action and sharing with them the reality of what the job really was. She proved her point by telling me how many candidates withdrew their applications after meeting her, not because of her personality or interview style but because they saw firsthand exactly what the job was about. Working in the casino industry for forty years, I can tell you our turnover rates in several areas were horrendous. Our goal was to reduce that number and, taking her lead, I directed that the beverage manager do something similar when he interviewed for servers. We asked candidates to turn up for their interviews in heels, which were a part of the dress code, and took them into our showroom, loaded up a tray of bottled water, and had them walk the perimeter four times. It might seem callous, uncaring, or even repugnant, but it was reality, and those who took the job never complained because they knew what the job was about before they even started. The caveat to all this is to make sure you follow my two examples by mimicking the worst realities of the job. And you do so with a lot of grace, explaining very clearly why you are conducting the interview the way you are and genuinely thanking them for partaking in the exercise. I cannot stress enough that it is important to ensure you do not humiliate or embarrass anyone. Also, asking if they would mind participating will tell you a great deal.

TIME FOR TEA!

Anyone who doesn't show a natural support of their team isn't a leader. They are, and likely deserve to be, simply standing alone.

If you can have more than one person interview your final three candidates, do it. As the senior vice president of a company with 1,500+ team members and over a dozen directors and vice presidents, I knew picking someone for the executive team who would fit well, perform well, and get the best out of their team was critical. Some called it a long day, and for the candidate, it was. By design. Being an executive for a single location with over a million square feet under the roof and nearly a quarter of a billion dollars in annual revenues meant long, grueling hours, working holidays, and missing putting your kids to bed. Directors would meet with their counterparts in groups of two or three, followed by being interviewed by the vice presidents one on one, and with me last. Once again, it was not a trick or attempt to catch anybody off guard, but I did want to see how they fared after such a tiring interview process and what their reactions were toward my questions about how their day had gone. I do not know that I always trusted anyone who said "I had a great time" or "It was really enjoyable" or "I loved meeting everyone." I had so much more respect for the lady who told me "My feet are killing me" and a gentleman who was quick to share that he was "Simply exhausted," knowing that if they were to join the team, that is exactly what they would have told me after a long day. So why not find out if they are truthful straightaway?

A part of the hiring process for that company was for me to sit at the head of the table and go around the room to see what each of the interviewers thought of the candidate, offering them the choices of *hire, pass,* or *put them on ice as a possible candidate.* I never shared my own opinion, and the rule was that we only hired if the room was unanimous in its decision. I did not always agree with them, and I will not say that as a team we did not make a couple of mistakes, but by and large there were very few decisions we regretted, and there is nothing better than telling the successful candidate that they were the unanimous choice of the people that they would be working with. It would be remiss of me not to add the lady who was hired unanimously and asked our vice president of operations three times "Now what is it you do, dear?" As they say in the South ... well, bless her heart!

Once you have made the job offer and the team member has accepted, it is time to really talk about the wonderful things that make their decision a good one and why you are so happy that they are taking a leap of faith and joining you. Being humble, warm, and welcoming costs you absolutely nothing. First impressions are everything. Share why *you* work for the company and why you stay. Talk about the culture of the team, your goals, your aspirations, and even your dreams and how they will fit in.

> **There is nothing better than telling the successful candidate that they were the unanimous choice.**

> *First impressions matter. Experts say we size up new people in somewhere between 30 seconds and two minutes.*
>
> **—ELLIOTT ABRAMS**

Let me go back for a moment and talk about the interview itself. Anyone who interviews a candidate from behind their desk, to me, is a fool. You are establishing very clearly your superiority, an elevated status, when you do not have to. Come around from behind your desk, and sit up at the very least at equal height from your interviewee. It sends a loud and clear message that you are not there to intimidate them, and you do not hold the upper hand, and that even though you are the person to make the hiring decision, they are to make a decision, too, and determine whether they want to join you on your journey at this company. It is only common courtesy and says so much about you, your company, and its culture if you make the person opposite you feel comfortable, welcomed, and wanted.

Have a copy of their résumé in your hand, but do not read from it. That tells them that you have only just picked it up, irrespective of whether that is true or not. Refer to what you remember, and ask for more detail. Read from a well-prepared and scripted list of questions that you have, and know who it is you are talking to well in advance.

In addition, it will disappoint your candidate if you do not know the answers to all the questions they will have. Smart candidates ask about opportunities for advancement, benefit packages, reviews, the company's culture, core values, who they are replacing, and why that person left. You do not have to, and maybe you should not be expected to, know or want to answer all the questions they may have, but honesty and clear answers are key. If you do not know the answer to a question they ask about benefits, promise that you will find out and make sure that you follow up. Even though they are indicating they will or have already accepted the job, it is a critical time to ask what concerns they might have between the day they're offered the job and their first day. Dig a little, and make sure that they are 100 percent comfortable and ready to go with the knowledge you or somebody else you delegate provides them. To the question about why somebody left the position that they now hold, if it was an involuntary separation, there truly is nothing wrong with telling the truth. If it was theft, attendance, substance abuse, poor work performance, attitude, or any other reason, simply respond, "Unfortunately, they were unable to live by our core values or the values of our culture here"—because that, in mostly all cases, is the truth.

> *I am convinced that nothing we do is more important than hiring and developing people. At the end of the day, you bet on people, not on strategies.*
>
> **—LAWRENCE BOSSIDY**

This HR quote comes from American author and former CEO of Allied Signal, later HomeWell. It portrays a notion key to successful HR management: the acknowledgment that workers are a business's most important resource.

A careful and in-depth onboarding experience is essential for both enticing and maintaining leading team members. Great HR leaders do not seek to fill spots, then forget about workers after they've spent a few months on the job. They choose applicants who they know will be an exceptional fit for the position, then help in their success by providing pertinent and useful training programs and consistently facilitating impactful collaboration within the business.

So now that you have picked your candidate, let us talk about onboarding. Rule number one for me is this: do not call this period a probationary period. It is not. It is simply a time for you to find out whether you are a fit for them and they for you. Let me stress that you being a fit for them is more important now than it ever has been. The fact is, rates of turnover are exponentially high, especially within the first ninety days of employment. The numbers must be a wake-up call for anyone in leadership. Sky Ariella with Zippia shared over two dozen statistics, including 31 percent of employees quitting within the first six months of starting a new job, an annual turnover rate of 57.3 percent (up from 42 percent in just six years). Ariella also claims 58 percent of employees would consider changing jobs for increased pay transparency, jumping to 70 percent for Gen Z.[7] Adding to the pain for employers, Kim Parker and Juliana Menasce Horowitz published an article for the Pew Research Center citing the majority of workers who quit a job in 2021 cite low pay, no opportunities for advancement, and feeling disrespected.[8]

Several years ago, we lost a good leader. On their first day they were shown their office and spent the morning cleaning out the desk that contained the personal items of their predecessor. The carpet was worn, the walls clearly needed a new coat of paint, but the greatest insult was the fact that we had not planned appropriately for their arrival, even forgetting to have ordered business cards. To some that might seem trivial, but it did teach me an everlasting lesson. Take the time to make sure, whether it is frontline or executive, that every new team member has what they need to be successful on the first day of the job. A note of welcome and a tour on their first day should be accompanied by an assurance that anything they need is theirs to have. You can't expect anyone to succeed if they don't have the right tools to do the job.

I learned about another horrifyingly missed opportunity when I spoke with an HR manager who had been with us only a few months

---

7   Larry Stybel, "Why 33 Percent of New Employees Quit in 90 Days," *Psychology Today*, March 3, 2019, https://www.psychologytoday.com/us/blog/platform-success/201903/why-33-percent-new-employees-quit-in-90-days.

8   Kim Parker and Juliana Menasce Horowitz, "Majority of Workers Who Quit a Job in 2021 Cite Low Pay, No Opportunities for Advancement, Feeling Disrespected," Pew Research Center, March 9, 2022, https://www.pewresearch.org/fact-tank/2022/03/09/majority-of-workers-who-quit-a-job-in-2021-cite-low-pay-no-opportunities-for-advancement-feeling-disrespected/.

and was responsible for onboarding other new team members. I asked her how she was settling in. True to the culture I was trying to promote of honesty and respectful candor, she responded how disappointed she was to find she had been walking through and down several hallways and corridors to a bathroom when there was one just a few feet from her office. Nobody, including me, had bothered to take the time to give her the courtesy of a full tour of our property.

In my mind, it is an absolute crime to go to the trouble of recruiting, interviewing, hiring, and making promises of a bright future to a candidate when you do not have the basic decency to be prepared for them to walk through your door for their first day of work. Onboarding is more than just about creating a list of information you wish to share with a new team member.

> *If you look for a shortcut, then you'll always find one. Build something incredible and embrace the formula to our future success. Set the standard for how you will intentionally direct your business after an immediate, emotional and unexpected transition.*
>
> **—DR. CHARLIE CULP, DMD**

I have seen managers, directors, and vice presidents turn up on their first day, looking their absolute best and eager to impress, only to be completely let down by what could easily be interpreted as a dereliction of basic respect and responsibility. How would you expect someone to feel if they park their car nowhere near where they should and walk through the door of their new office to see pictures hung by their predecessor? How do you expect them to feel if they need to empty the desk of somebody else's personal belongings? How would they feel if they don't have all the basic tools and equipment they need? How will they react when they are unable to offer anyone a business card or, worse yet, cannot log on to their own computer? What if, on top of that, they do not have a directory available to them so they can call someone for assistance? All these examples are so simple and only require common decency and a little planning.

Percentage of team members who will change jobs and simply leave you within ninety days:

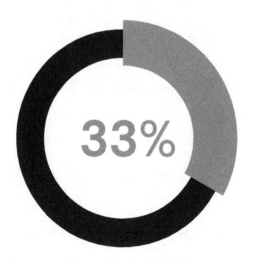

TIME FOR TEA!

If you are in a leadership role, enjoy the skills of leaders who report to you, and don't let anyone dump a problem on your desk and walk away. They have an obligation to bring you the problem and one or more workable solutions.

Your job is to pick the best and fully support their actions.

In other words: "Don't leave a **** on my desk and leave me with just the bad smell!"

Now let's flip the coin and imagine the impression made when your new hire enters the office, smells fresh paint, looks down at a clean desk where there is a welcome note from you along with a freshly printed box of business cards and a directory of who to call if they need anything. Take the time to predict and think about anything they may need all the way from paperclips and a stapler to notepads and fresh ink in their printer. Tell or show them exactly where the bathroom, coffee, breakroom, and office supplies are and who their go-to person is, especially if that's you. Think about what that says about you, your company, your culture, and how you will expect them to welcome anybody *they* hire.

In addition, you want to consider how you communicate to the rest of your team about who has just arrived. Could anything be worse than people inquiring, "So who's the new guy?" If you can't do it yourself, find somebody to schedule time to introduce a new team member to as many people as possible. You should also email your entire team with the announcement about their arrival date, their position, who they report to, and their role within the company. Adding some brief information about where they came from, their talents and skills, and why you hired them can serve you well. Finally, organize yourself to have all state and federal paperwork ready in a package that might combine your payday schedule, specific policies, training expectations (fire drill or CPR, etc.), and a copy of your handbook.

Onboarding, for so many reasons, should last for the full scope of time a team member is with you. They should be constantly learning more about the company, the culture, who they are working for, who they are working with, and who they serve, as well as the evolving nature and direction of the company itself. I have always advocated that to be successful, you have to do an outstanding job of onboarding new team members and ensuring they have everything they need to be and want to stay with you. Let us not forget that they are also a walking advertisement for you and your company brand. They will tell everyone they know how much they love or hate their job or how you missed something as simple as ordering them business cards or telling them where the restroom is. Final words on this subject: done well, onboarding can ensure you have made a wonderful first impression that will last forever and differentiate you and your company from the competition.

There's no shame in recognizing that the skills of a responsible leader are akin to those of a master chef. Perfection and the need for recognition of excellent work are in their DNA. Combine those traits with the need to grow your business through personal recommendations and online reviews, and the pressure you place upon yourself is ruthless.

In the same vein, business owners, executives, and chefs also have little time for chit-chat, as one award-winning professional shared when I was recruiting for her. Asked what environment and leadership style a candidate might expect, she delivered a crisp response without hesitation or apology: "Speak to me in context. And if your dog died—I'm sorry, but I don't have time to cry with you right now."

> Done well, onboarding can ensure you have made a wonderful first impression that will last forever.

Undoubtedly the number of candidates for that role would shrink immediately after I posted an accurate job description for the role. But who cares? My job was to find the perfect candidate who would fit *her* needs, personality, and, let's be honest … blunt style. The truth is, though, that to this day, she is one of the most admired leaders I've worked with and has a genuinely generous heart. She just truly doesn't have the time to spend her energies on anyone but her patients during the time that's dedicated to them.

There's no shame in being who you are. But if you expect your office manager to tell a candidate that their owner might "come unglued if the flow of clients unravels" or that "sometimes you're going to feel unappreciated or go unnoticed for a job well done," you're probably very, very mistaken.

Why won't they tell the truth? Quite simple. *Loyalty.*

Asking your office manager to share what you're really like to work with can be a half-baked and completely unrealistic notion, *unless* you take the genuinely sincere step and reassure them that telling the truth is the right thing to do. Go ahead and say, "I'm impatient, demanding, sometimes curt, and I hate long fingernails, and I'm totally comfortable with you sharing that with your candidates. Let's get the right person in here who understands our culture and our core values and is comfortable with the expectations."

Otherwise? Sure, they'll tell a candidate that you're extremely generous, well respected, highly skilled, and have clients that love you. What they cannot and will not share is your tendency to be curt, avoid eye contact first thing in the morning, forget your birthday, fail to recognize that you're sick, or drop the f-bomb occasionally when everything is screwed up.

Why would you put them in that unenviable position?

Forget for a moment the high cost of your office manager plowing through a hundred applications and interviewing a dozen applicants. As someone who has recruited, interviewed, and hired for all levels of position across the country, I needed to know what your foibles, personal traits, loves, and hates are. Sometimes, soon after starting a candidate interview, I would think of the business owner I represented and state: "I'm going to do my best to talk you out of this job, because I don't want to have to interview someone again in three months!"

I start by finding out how sensitive a candidate is. I ask how important recognition and rewards are to them, what makes them leave a job, and how demanding they consider *too* demanding. Best of all, I can say, "The boss has a short fuse and has no time for chit-chat. Knowing all that, are you still interested?" Only then will I share the benefits of the job.

One last advantage of using a third party is this: Candidates don't have to like a consultant who's hiring for someone else. They simply must really want the job, know who they are working for, and feel comfortable enough to move forward.

So that's why I advocate for using a third party. The alternative is to do it yourself or train your leaders on the *how* to hire. Leave it to your office manager and you might be asking "So, why did she leave?" When that happens, you don't really expect to hear the truth—do you?

Let me add to the end of this chapter by stating a few simple rules you must follow:

1. Make sure every piece of paperwork required of a new hire is completed thoroughly and checked carefully for accuracy and completion. Over the years, I have completed many audits of personnel files and found missing information on I-9s, missing handbook acknowledgment forms that should be signed, and witnessed and signed acknowledgments of the job offer itself. Each is the responsibility of either a leader or the owner of every business. I will touch on it in another chapter, but the importance of not only how an I-9 is completed but also where and for how long it is stored is important, unless you don't mind being fined up to tens

of thousands of dollars for your lack of attention to this federally required paperwork.

2. Depending on the position you've filled, you can do several things as a leader to help positively affect a team member's onboarding experience and their first day at work. A rule of thumb is to ensure you are consistent, because if you are not and you do not do for one what you have done for another, you will do more damage than good. At the very least, a personal introduction and a tour of the facility is warranted. Putting out a memo of welcome with a short bio of the new team member goes a long way. If you have what we commonly refer to as "swag" (i.e., T-shirts, ball caps, pens, or other giveaways that you would normally give a client), share one or two with your new team member. Best of all, in my opinion, is the personal handwritten note I keep mentioning, signed by you and stating how pleased and grateful you are that they have chosen to join you and your company. This goes a long, long way.

Feedback is a gift. Ideas are the currency of our next success. Let people see you value both feedback and ideas.
—JIM TRINKA AND LES WALLACE

I will end this chapter with one last idea that I think works well for new team members. Mark your calendar for seven, thirty, sixty, and ninety days from the team member's date of hire. Your first meeting after the seventh day should be casual and preferably over a cup of coffee, away from your office and theirs. Make sure they are relaxed which, of course, means making sure that you are. Open the conversation with a simple "How's it going?"

Include these follow-up questions:

- Tell me truthfully, did we make a good enough effort to make you feel welcomed, but more importantly, anticipated?

- Tell me your first impressions, good and bad?

- Who is helping you, and who could help you more?

- What else do you need to succeed?

- I know that it is probably too early to tell, but are you glad you made this decision?

And finally—the number one question that is a *must*-ask: "Are you happy?"

Finish the conversation by making a promise that you will follow up on anything they shared that needs attention, and restate your commitment to their happiness and success.

Do this exact same exercise after thirty days, but this time you should add some of your own first impressions and observations along with any feedback you have received. This is your opportunity to identify and applaud great results or identify where the team member may be failing and, at worst, may not succeed or meet your expectations. Use the opportunity to share any positive praise your new hire deserves. Top of mind should be their efforts to adapt to your culture, how well they are working with others, and any positive feedback from others within or outside of your company.

Check in a third time after sixty days with more emphasis on performance, promises made and promises kept on both sides. Once again, use the time to reemphasize where this team member is meeting your expectations or failing them.

At the ninety-day review, if the candidate is turning out not to be a poor fit, document their wins, where there might be room for improvement, and the time frame left for you to be reassured that you made a good hiring decision.

> *Clients do not come first. Team members come first.*
> **—RICHARD BRANSON**

Richard Branson's business philosophy that people are our greatest asset was not just created to influence his workers. He truly believes team members should be given top priority. He has established a nonhierarchical, open, family-like culture in all his organizations, an atmosphere in which individuals like to come and work. Branson preserves business honor within each of his Virgin company brands. If your team is happy and enjoying its work, it will remain productive. Accordingly, the customers will enjoy their experience with your business.

I have my own philosophical thoughts about team member satisfaction. I'm unshakable in my belief that if you genuinely take care of your team members and make them the most important asset you have, they will take care of your clients, customers, or patients. In turn, those paying for your services and products will take care of you and your company. I hope you see the obvious connection to you being taken care of. At this point, you now have the ability and the funds to keep the cycle going.

TIME FOR TEA!

Your handbook is a critical document that will very clearly communicate your culture and the level of respect you have for your team members and give them an opportunity to discover whether they feel motivated or uneasy after reading it.

CHAPTER 6

AN UNTAPPED POOL OF TALENT

tal·ent

/ˈtalənt/

a natural aptitude or skill

Regardless of the latest statistics that report the number of unemployed Americans, there continues to be a huge gap between the quality of applicants and the demands of the decision makers. Open positions in some fields frequently exceed the number of résumés on quality employment websites. Looking for an experienced dental assistant, CFO, or any skilled team member with experience on Indeed, Zip Recruiter, or Monster can be frustrating to an owner and to anyone who has the responsibility of recruiting.

I enjoyed an article written by Kelsey Moriarty that clearly highlights many of the challenges facing anyone responsible for hiring. Eighty-one percent of talent acquisition professionals indicate that attracting top talent has become more challenging, and 62 percent say their top recruiting priority right now is increasing the quality of hire.[9] Many of us continually struggle to find qualified candidates to fill a variety of positions. That challenge appears to be getting worse, not better. Best of all, department/team leaders and business owners who find themselves short-staffed often look to human resources and say, "What's the problem? What's slowing you down from finding me people?"

Employers frequently become frustrated when the perfect and experienced new team member doesn't make it to their ninety-day review. How could this be? All I can say to that is before you point the finger at them, ask yourself first: What did I do wrong? It's not unreasonable to think it was all their fault, but taking the time to perform exit interviews and an introspective look at what you did to ensure their success is time well spent.

What if we've been overlooking a pool of talent because we're placing too much emphasis on the wrong cognitive skills? What if we started the search by putting quality ahead of experience?

Former US military service members often struggle to find gainful employment despite having so much to offer the workforce. Veterans frequently struggle to find opportunities to make the most of their abilities and find work that provides stability and job satisfaction. I'm not suggesting that employers are opposed to hiring veterans. But do we seek them out as a top resource? Can an argument be made that the term *veteran* generates an image of a uniformed, well decorated, rigidly thinking retiree who only knows how to fly an F-16, live in a bunker, and take orders?

---

9   Kelsey Moriarty, "ICYMI: The Top 10 States Employers Should Know About Hiring in the Current Labor Market," October 5, 2022, https://www.jobvite.com/blog/talent-market-insights/icymi-the-top-10-stats-employers-should-know-about-hiring-in-the-current-labor-market/.

> *One machine can do the work of fifty*
> *ordinary men. No machine can do the*
> *work of one extraordinary man.*
>
> **—ELBERT HUBBARD**

Elbert Hubbard was an American writer, publisher, artist, and philosopher from the nineteenth century. His quote proves that a great leader recognizes that every team member has the potential to offer a unique set of skills that could be extremely beneficial to the company. Leadership that consistently acknowledges this diversity of skills motivates every individual team member to continue to strengthen their quality of work, effectively increasing the morale of the workforce.

Military enlistment teaches critical skills that employers desire with intangible attributes that are rare. Who wouldn't want to hire someone who instinctively understands and respects a disciplined lifestyle, is adaptable, embraces teamwork, is naturally creative, thinks quickly, and is trained to find solutions? Most have specialized skills developed through training to discover their strengths. They genuinely understand the need for commitment, have the ability to accept direction, and probably have the best understanding of reliability and being on time for work!

Some time ago, I started the process of purposely making a job posting attractive to veterans. Employers are tired of the time and expenses related to the hiring process. The investment in training can easily be a worthwhile use of time and effort. When I mentioned this to one of our most demanding clients, she immediately took to the idea. I think employers are figuring it out and agree that we should put skills before experience and recruit these valuable and available talents. Unemployment figures further support why hiring veterans is even more attractive. With a rate of 5.2 percent unemployment, it's clear that many are looking for work, with 56 percent falling between the ages of twenty-five and fifty-four.

There are job placement organizations who can match veterans to opportunities that will suit their needs and abilities. This is one of the simplest and most effective ways to ensure that your job opening is seen by veterans who would fit the role you're hiring for. Before you reach out, be clear on your expectations and evaluate what you can provide your candidate. Veterans may have physical or mental disabilities. If necessary, is your office or workspace accessible, or do you provide health insurance that includes benefits for physical *and* mental health? This is an important consideration to think through.

TIME FOR TEA!

Budgets serve as the story you must tell based on the best resources and information you have at the time of creating them. If a major piece of equipment needs to be replaced, you're going to replace it regardless of its budget status. I look for the ability in a leader to be able to share how they arrived at their numbers—the confidence and knowledge to have the budget tell the story of where they're going. It's my job to help them to the best of my ability.

CHAPTER 7

REVIEWS

re·view

/rəˈvyo͞o/

a report on or evaluation of a subject or past events

If you asked me to think of one word that sums up complete dismay, frustration, a sense of overwhelmingness, and sheer reticence in the role of any leader, it would be the word "reviews." Performance reviews, annual reviews, onboarding reviews, ninety-day reviews; they all add up to work but are often shied away from or ignored by even the best of leaders. Team members generally dread the review process and work to avoid it at all costs, especially if they know their leader is not going to get the job done properly or on time. Let me go on record and say that reviews have the potential of being a tremendous tool for building a lasting and motivated team with excellent morale versus a negative and degrading experience for everyone. Sadly, the review process for most companies, large and small, is broken, unrealistic, unreliable, or nonexistent. Or all the above.

> *Performance management should focus on strengths and help team members develop these, rather than weaknesses.*
>
> **—SHOURYA CHAKRAVARTY**

Most leaders are oblivious to the fact that reviews can very easily be a gift to an attorney who is defending a team member accusing you of discrimination and unfair or constructive dismissal. Although I recommend anything in a review reflect only the past twelve months' performance, an eager attorney will happily subpoena every review you have written and use all the positive remarks and ratings against you in support of what they will defend to be an exemplary team member. There is as much danger in a poorly worded positive review as there is in a poorly worded negative review. Your job is to stick to the facts and create an objective, constructive, and timely document that encompasses the performance of your team member for the full period of the review. It is important that you do not fall into the trap of rating somebody higher than they deserve simply because they have improved over the last three months of a twelve-month evaluation. The same applies to rating somebody poorly who has been a disappointment for the latter part of the year.

Leaders often do themselves a great disservice by making it known how much they dislike the review process and not rating team members accordingly. I am agitated when I meet supervisors and leaders who openly share that they do not give fives based on the reasoning that no one is perfect. Quite candidly, I think that's hogwash. Seriously, if your review process has a five as your top score and someone deserves it, why wouldn't you award them with that recognition? It is an absolute insult to rate someone a four who deserves a five. And do not think that word does not get around that you are a leader who scores this way. You are basically, in turn, telling everyone that they will never make the grade, and in turn, they will never try hard to be a five. Why bother, right?

And then, there are other leaders who are, quite frankly, afraid of delivering a bad review, so they overrate a team member who simply does not deserve it. This does nothing but set the team member up for failure and provide them with everything they need to let you down for another year and put you in a position where corrective action is almost impossible. If you are too afraid to tell your team member that their performance has been less than stellar, you simply shouldn't be a part of the review process. Learn how to deliver bad news in a way that is motivational, supportive, and, most importantly, genuinely realistic.

If you are doing a review that's designed to be a wake-up call and put a team member on notice because you're less than happy with their performance, it would be more beneficial for you to first determine whether this team member should still be a part of your organization. There is simply no point in writing a horrible review that denigrates and demotivates someone and makes clear the writing on the wall. You are better off creating an action plan versus a review or, if necessary, allow yourself to go ahead and separate them from the company. On the flip side, a well-written factually based and motivational review that is delivered with compassion and the genuine reassurance that you have faith in the person sitting in front of you will have more than just successful results. Trust me on this one.

Here is a little story for you. Several years ago, I delivered a review to a leader who I had promoted. Several hours later that evening, my telephone rang. It was the same leader. I am not even kidding when I say he started with "you bastard" as his opening engagement. When I asked him what was going on, he responded with, "That was the worst review I have ever received; I didn't get a pay raise, and yet I walked out of your office and felt like a million dollars." I have shared that story many times over the years because it meant a lot to me, and I think to him also. I was able to be honest with him without destroying his ability to perform until he finally made the grade and earned his raise the following year.

Keep in mind that most of today's millennials need feedback. They prefer to receive it often, which emphasizes their need for regular feedback throughout the year, ensuring that when you do meet with them on their hiring anniversary, there are no surprises, good or bad. Not everyone is the same, and you need to treat people as individuals when it relates to communicating their goals, progress, and performance. It's not difficult to figure out what works best for someone. Ask. Some will enjoy a regular chat, and others not so much. Tailoring your communication needs to match theirs is an indication that you are thinking about them personally and professionally and making the review process work the way they want it to.

> *Feedback, when given well, should not alienate the receiver of the feedback, but should motivate them to perform better.*
> **—M. O., MANAGER, FORTUNE 500 COMPANY**

The biggest issue with reviews is how the accuracy, fairness, and timeliness of delivery plays into the morale of your team members. Thousands of supervisors, manager leaders, senior leaders, directors, and business owners are, quite frankly, untrained and unprepared for the complexity of completing a "good review." In addition, the number of reviews that need to be completed on a regular basis can be overwhelming. Think of a restaurant manager who is responsible for evaluating the performance of head chefs, assistant head chefs, sous chefs, prep cooks, dishwashers, front-of-house managers, supervisors, wait staff, bussers, front desk hosts, valet parking attendants, and more. Within the average-sized quality chain steakhouse, there are likely sixty or more team members. That requires the restaurant manager to be completing a minimum of one or two reviews every week, and that is not even accounting for turnover in a highly volatile industry.

The question for that leader is this:

- Do I conduct the reviews by myself, knowing I do not have hands-on knowledge of the performance expectations of every team member? Or do I delegate?

If he or she chooses to delegate, they are likely giving the job to someone who has even less training and experience with completing reviews. Adding to the problem is the number of different reviews you need to be familiar with. You cannot rate someone in customer service if they are back of house and don't interact with guests. In the same vein, you cannot possibly have similar reviews for a sous chef and the wait staff. So, even if the manager does decide to delegate reviews, they will still be responsible for signing off on the ratings, the verbiage, and the inevitable requests for an increase in pay.

Let's return to the issue of not being trained to complete reviews. Poorly worded ratings and scores with rushed reviews that have not been thought out, followed by ill-conceived goals, can do more than just kill the morale of a team member. They can most certainly also land you in hot water and bring you up against a potentially unpleasant letter from an attorney. A team member who does not feel their review is fair can easily claim discrimination, whether it was intended or not. Reviews are a classic case of perception; there are different views on both sides. The supervisor or manager may feel that the team member has not performed to their full potential, but how do they share that information and motivate the team member to do better for the next review? And to do so while leaving the team member with a sense of dignity and respect is not an easy feat. Too many reviews contain subjective rather than objective wording, and that is dangerous. Putting anything in writing that communicates that someone could be more pleasant, smile more, be easier to get along with, or dress more neatly can potentially get you into a situation where you must defend yourself. Objective observations might include encouraging your direct report to work on how they greet and thank your guests, be more receptive to criticism and feedback, and adhere to your company's dress code.

I also want to touch on three review-related topics that truly make my head spin and a third I'm absolutely convinced is a sure-fire way to disenfranchise both team members and leaders. The first is a common mistake bigger than I could have imagined before I started consulting and requires team members to self-evaluate. Why in heavens name would anyone ask a team member to rate their own performance? To start with, it wreaks of laziness and communicates that the reviewer doesn't know, hasn't got the time, or simply doesn't care enough to complete the review themselves. What a horrible position the team member is put in! If they rate themselves a five, will they be seen as arrogant or too self-aggrandiz-

> Too many reviews contain subjective rather than objective wording, and that is dangerous.

ing? What if the reviewer disagrees? How well does that conversation go? Conversely, the team member has low self-esteem and rates themselves a two. Do you know they have low self-worth, or do you suspect that they know more than you do about their low performance? There are several variations of how this can go horribly wrong and, trust me, it will—for both sides.

The second sin is to have coworkers review or rate each other. I've seen firsthand the devastating disruption caused to what once was a cohesive team before this tactic was used. It *might* work with large groups of people, but if the plan is to have people like and trust each other, run away from this idea as fast as you can. The impact it can have on a team of five people—and yes, I've seen it done—is catastrophic. Someone who might not be in the clique is saddled with low ratings. Meanwhile, the bully and the BFFs get high scores from everyone. Peer reviews are about the least constructive plan in the book. I beg anyone who is using this method to stop immediately.

The third is the double whammy, where you are sure to kill the morale of pretty much everyone with the rating system itself. Once again, I've witnessed this firsthand after asking a consultancy client how the policy for his company increases worked. The COO proudly told me that it was a fair and rewarding policy that recognized everyone with a final scoring method that rated team members one through five. Okay so far. Next, he proceeded to share the policy for increases. "We never give anyone a review without an increase," he said, looking at me quizzically as my eyes furrowed, wondering why I would have a problem with this generous philosophy. "Our best team members with a five rating get a 5 percent increase, and that's great for morale. We like to reward our top performers." As I processed what he was telling me, I immediately asked what the lowest increase was and predicted his answer. "One percent, but like I said—everyone gets something." Here is where I had to share with him how completely insane I thought his policy was. I walked him through the worst-case scenario. The low-performing team member, instead of earning an increase of zero—which is potentially what they deserve—is given 1 percent. With an entry-level position, a team member is hired at nineteen dollars per hour. He would be rewarding them with nineteen cents per hour, which by the easiest of calculations meant that the increase was worth an additional $380 per year for two thousand hours worked, moving them from an annual income of $38,000 to $38,380. You can see where this is going, I'm sure. After taxes, the team member walks home with about $305 or $5.85 a week. Now, consider the morale of any leader who has to deliver the paltry increase of less than $6.00. WHAM! Two demotivated team members for the price of one. And now word is out. Both the team member *and* the leader are grumbling to others. Way to go! Anyone who is earning in the region of nineteen dollars per hour should get nothing less than a fifty-cent-per-hour / $1,000-per-year increase—that is, *if* they have earned it.

1% – $0.50 – 3% expense versus retention. You be the judge.

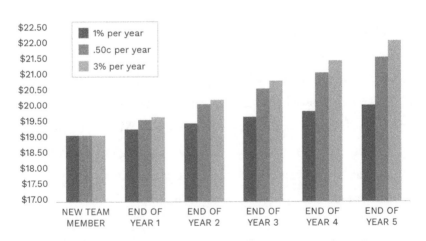

TIME FOR TEA!

Nothing that is important to your business should be limited to a skill set that just one person on the team has. Always think ahead and plan for what happens if that one team member leaves. Without planning, people leave—you and chaos.

There are also those leaders who prefer to follow the guidance of companies that have done away with reviews altogether. Several top Fortune 500 companies have opted out of reviews. The danger with this methodology is justifying why team member A received an increase that team member B did not, without any documentation to back it up.

I think you also miss the opportunity to provide positive feedback, gratitude, and an acknowledgment of good work when it is due versus a verbal thank you once a year and a pay increase to a good performer. You also miss out on providing feedback to poor performers.

If you're not performing reviews (and I would advocate having them in writing), consider the following:

- How does a team member know they are on the right track for success within your organization?

- How will they know what their goals are for the next year to be successful?

- How will they know if they are working toward the promotion they have always wanted?

- How are they supposed to understand why a few extra dollars turn up on their next paycheck if they don't understand how it might not match what they were expecting?

The creation of an excellent review, if you are starting from scratch, requires structure and good planning to ensure effectiveness.

Start by evaluating your team member on any core value or mission statement of your company. Well-written core values can be the true basis for how you think about approaching an individual's evaluation. If, for instance, one of your core values is "always assume positive intent," but the supervisor in question jumps to conclusions and is quick to point a finger, it is easy to see how to approach this segment and score it accordingly. How much weight this section and others have toward the total scoring depends on how you value each of them, which, in turn, should reflect the value each has to your company and its success.

For the next section, I would suggest evaluating your team member on five key components of their job description, asking yourself if they have met or exceeded expectations. This is a good time to point out that just meeting expectations should never really be enough and certainly should not warrant an increase. Put a different way, the cost of doing business for you increases on a regular basis, and you must work harder to make ends meet and create a profit. If your business just meets standards and does not improve and show a willingness to change and evolve as time goes by, you certainly do not expect your customers to spend more with you—ergo, you do not get a raise either.

Key performance indicators should relate to measurable and, once again, objective goals you have set for either an individual or the overall team for a review period. These are easy to score in as much as the results should speak for themselves and the scoring falls into place naturally.

According to KPI.org:

Key Performance Indicators (KPIs) are the critical (key) indicators of progress toward an intended result. KPIs provide a focus for strategic and operational improvement, create an analytical basis for decision-making and help focus attention on what matters most.

Managing with the use of KPIs includes setting targets (the desired level of performance) and tracking progress against that target. Managing with KPIs often means working to improve leading indicators that will later drive lagging benefits. Leading indicators are precursors of future success; lagging indicators show how successful the organization was at achieving results in the past.[10]

Finally, I tend to prefer a section that speaks to skills and standards. This can include multiple areas to evaluate performance.

Here are just a few of the measurable expectations that you can set:

- Timeliness of work

- Ability to prioritize

- Whether or not the team member has the capability for independent decision-making

- Dependability—in every sense

- Consciousness of waste and cost control

- Accurateness in their work

- How well they work under pressure

- What their interactive skills are with your customers and their coworkers

Needless to say, but once again, there is a need to be able to back up and, wherever possible, notate specifics—whether you are giving positive or negative feedback.

Put aside time well in advance of the review. I like to think of this date on the calendar that marks the team member's work anniversary as their work birthday. That does not mean to say it *must* be a cause for celebration, but it does have to be just as important for you to do a good job of recognizing the date as it is to the team member who

---

10   "What Is a Key Performance Indicator (KPI)?" KPI.org, accessed December 1, 2022, https://www.kpi.org/kpi-basics/.

expects, and quite frankly deserves, to be recognized for completing another year of service with you. Remember, team members have choices, regardless of what the unemployment numbers are.

Finding the time and space to complete a review can be a challenge. To do the job properly, set more than ample time aside, uninterrupted and without any distractions at all, barring an emergency. There is nothing more disrespectful to a team member who is listening to you talk about their performance—good or bad—than when you allow yourself to be disturbed by someone who has a question that could wait. Do what you must to ensure that your meeting is private. You will also need to go in with a clear head and no biases, remembering that if you are not in the right frame of mind, that will overflow and clearly show through during the review.

A good tip for any leader is to keep notes throughout the year for each team member and refer to the notes when you are completing reviews. I use sticky notes for easy reference for notes I should look back on during review time. Just adding the incident, a date, and the names of anyone involved will help you remember an occasion that helps justify the high or low rating for a review. Obviously, every note needs to be, again, objective versus subjective. The value of the notes can be great when you are trying to remember not only the good work your team member has done for the past twelve months but also the specifics. A team member will respect you tremendously if you detail the exact occasions with names and dates. For instance, you might refer to a telephone call or letter you received from a guest that praised a specific team member for a high level of service. "I rated you a five for how well you react under pressure. When Mr. Bothersome called and berated you about the poor level of service he received back in March, you did such a wonderful job of turning a bad situation into a great one just by being sincere, staying calm, and reassuring him that you would address his complaints. He's still a client of ours today because of you!" Now *that's* motivational.

Make sure you use good grammar and write legibly. If you do not feel you can do that, enter everything via a preset computer program or template. If your handwriting is bad, you might want to take the time and either write in all block capitals or, again, use your keyboard if possible. Sloppy or illegible writing when trying to deliver a review speaks volumes and will not earn you any fans.

When it comes time to delivering the review, you need to give serious thought, once again, to finding an ideal time and space where you can speak with your team member without interruption and ensure that you put enough time aside for feedback. Do not rush the process. If you are using your office, avoid sitting behind your desk and, instead, sit beside the team member you're about to review. This puts you on an even keel and removes an unnecessary perception of superiority that you do not need. It is already established that you are the top dog in this meeting, and you do not need to position yourself in a way that ruins any chance of open dialogue. Even the smallest detail can make a difference. Turn off your cell phone and, if you have an opportunity, make sure that everyone knows you cannot be interrupted unless there is an emergency. Simply put, this occasion, as I have stated before, is *all* about the team member, not you.

Over the years, I have made it a point to read reviews to my team members and not provide them with a copy until the very end of the meeting. Bad leaders shove the review in front of the team member, ask them to read it, and then ask if they have any feedback. If that is how you handle a review, you should expect nothing but negative emotions. By reading the review aloud, you can convey exactly what you mean simply by the tone of your voice and how you emphasize the importance of individual sections. It's also another gesture that makes the interactive process personal. Let me say it again. It's *all* about the team member and not about you.

As a good example, think of how the following sentence, if simply read, might be interpreted. By placing the emphasis on certain words, the team member can take away a completely different understanding of what you are attempting to say:

I hope you understand that I believe in your ability to be one of the most productive team members that we have at this location.

I hope *you understand* that I believe in your ability to be one of the most productive team members that we have at this location.

I hope you understand that *I believe in your ability* to be one of the most productive team members that we have at this location.

I hope you understand that I believe in your ability to be *one of the most productive* team members that we have at this location.

I hope you understand that I believe in your ability to be one of the most productive team members that we have *at this location.*

Remember, it's not what you say—but *how* you say it. Your tone of voice and how you emphasize particular words or phrases is profoundly important.

Delivering less-than-stellar reviews, of course, is a challenge and requires a real set of skills.

Wise leaders create an environment and culture that allows for open dialogue regardless of how good or bad the review is. This should be a moment of truth for you just as much as it is for the team member. Many leaders believe they are good at what they do and that their team members like them. And even though that can be true, the same cannot always be said about their leadership style.

Annual reviews are an optimum time to check in on certain things:

- Ask for and receive truthful feedback about *your own* performance over the last year.

- Ask what hurdles were present.

- Ask whether they felt they received the support of everyone, including you.

- Ask if they had the tools to succeed and how they feel you could have been a better leader.

Their answers will speak volumes. It will be your job to earn their trust in providing you with this critical feedback if you want to be a leader people will follow and stay with. Another key question for any team member is "Would you recommend working here to a friend?" Regardless of any of the answers to the above, it is fine to ask them to back up their comments.

Earlier, I mentioned that some companies have determined that doing away with reviews altogether is a good idea. However, I disagree with that notion, although I do believe there is a compromise that can work well for a leader who has multiple team members reporting directly to them. This might not work for everyone in every situation or every type of company, but for some, it could be perfect.

If you believe you could spare fifteen to thirty minutes every month for your team members, I will advocate there is a process that could truly benefit you both. The concept is simple. Once a month, choose a time and space where you can speak with them uninterrupted. Find out what your team member is working on, if they are having any challenges, and what support they need. Both of you should take notes and be expected to keep them ready to share when you meet again. Document and share any feedback that is relevant to the team member's performance, once again highlighting the positive and outlining areas for improvement. Set short-term goals that are both reasonable and achievable. Discuss them and make sure you agree on the timing as well as anything that is needed to achieve a successful outcome.

The next step is to compare your calendars and commit to a time and place where you can meet again and repeat the process. I cannot stress enough that if you cannot commit to this concept, then do not even start it. This is a commitment you will need to make for a full year and beyond. At the end of twelve months, you should have twelve pages of notes that document every conversation, every challenge, every directive, and all the goals that have been set. Reading through them, you will have a clear picture of exactly what has been accomplished. At that point, it should be easy to make an objective decision as to whether this team member has earned a pay increase or promotion. The beauty of this process is the commitment to communication and the lack of surprises at year end, and the bond that you will build with each other comes with the benefits of mutual trust, support, and understanding.

Just remember that whatever tool you use to evaluate your team members, you must follow these rules:

- Be honest.

- Be objective.

- Be timely.

- And perhaps more importantly, listen and be open to honest and objective feedback.

It never ceases to amaze me how little thought and research goes into the answer behind a standard question commonly posed during the initial hiring process: "How much does this position pay?" Many times, the response comes after some hesitation. "Well, I think probably somewhere between fourteen and sixteen dollars." I am always amazed that this response appears out of thin air. The truth is, the only reference point most employers have is what they are paying everyone else who holds a similar position and title. Combine that out-of-thin-air number with the knowledge that some team members being used to gauge an estimate for the wage of the new position have not had a review or pay increase, sometimes for several years, and you'll realize the chances of filling this position quickly, or at all, with a good candidate are very slim. I am positive that employers simply do not do their homework and research to discover what the going rate for the position they wish to fill truly is. It would take only a few moments to look at any one of the numerous recruitment websites to know that their estimate is off. When faced with the truth, they realize this will have a ripple effect on their existing team, and they are faced with either raising pay for those team members or risking to pay a new team member more than everyone else. That can cause its own set of problems.

> *Under the National Labor Relations Act (NLRA or the Act), "Team members have the right to communicate with other team members at their workplace about their wages. Wages are a vital term and condition of employment, and discussions of wages are often preliminary to organizing or other actions for mutual aid or protection."*
> **—NRLB.GOV**

With team members protected against repercussions for sharing wage information with one another, it likely won't be long before everyone finds out you have hired someone at a higher rate of pay. That leaves you with the unenviable task of having to justify that decision. Now, of course you can make a legitimate claim of more experience or a wider range of skills, but that does not satisfy anyone who has worked for you for several years and will claim discrimination or simple bias and unfairness. Remember, perception is reality!

Morale, of course, will tank, and even correcting the situation by giving raises will not replace the lack of faith and trust people will have in you going forward. Usually what ends up happening is that the employer sticks to the low pay range that matches what everybody else is making and posts for the position, hoping for the best.

The results are predictable: several unqualified, inexperienced, and totally unsuitable applications hit your desk, and you hope and pray you get lucky and find someone willing to earn less than they should. That leads to yet another ripple effect. One of two things is likely

Remember, perception is reality!

to happen. Either one or more of your team will figure out that they can earn more elsewhere and will leave en masse or, at the very least, your new team member will not last long.

You can also learn a lot by not advertising the pay range for the position. Consider this method as an alternative to finding out what the position should pay but also to finding a candidate who is likely to stay with you for a long time. We will use an entry-level position, perhaps a receptionist, as our example. Post the ad for the position, and be clear about the minimum required experience and skill set. Interview only those who meet your minimum standards. At the end of the interview, explain why you have not advertised what you are willing to pay by using this reasoning:

Consider a candidate who is looking for a job and requires fifteen dollars an hour just to make ends meet; they will accept the job offer at thirteen dollars just so that they can go home and say to their girlfriend, boyfriend, mother, father, or best friend, "Hey, I got a job. It pays only thirteen dollars an hour, but I got a job! Don't worry, I'll keep looking until I find a fifteen-dollar-per-hour position."

I probably do not have to explain what happens next.

At the end of the interview, I explain the scenario outlined above, and I say, "Tell me what the right number is that I need to pay you for you to immediately say yes and give me somewhat of an assurance that if everything else you expect from us works out well, you will stay for the long term." Your job then is to assess the value of the candidate who says eighteen dollars per hour when you have team members with similar responsibilities who earn less. At that point, it is decision time.

The simple lessons learned from all this should be the following:

- Regularly review and evaluate your team. Communicate!

- Be aware of what the market is paying for these positions. Stay competitive.

- Don't insult anyone with a 1 percent increase. It's laughably unfunny.

- Do the right thing, and pay people what they're worth, not what you can get away with. That's a reputation you don't want.

TIME FOR TEA!

Before you print a single copy of your handbook, add a statement that speaks to how it is a live document that can change based on the needs of your customers, clients, patients, or guests. But more importantly, to avoid poor morale and accusations of being a hypocrite, it will serve you well to think of yourself as someone who should live by the policies and culture outlined within it too.

CHAPTER 8

THE SLIPPERY SLOPE OF SALARIES

---

sal·a·ry

/ ˈsal-rē /

a fixed compensation paid regularly

Choosing whether to pay your new hire a wage or a salary? What are the pros and cons? Who benefits and why?

The easy answers aren't necessarily the right ones. The advantages of having a salaried team member are easy to understand and appreciate. You can budget easily, set variable schedules to match your needs, and expect more hours of work when the going gets tough. A salaried team member is exempt and is not going to earn a dime for working any overtime. Let me add one piece of advice here. Please don't act without honor. There is nothing worse than seeing an owner lowball a team member with a promotion, a paltry salary, and an unreasonable schedule. Of course, when the workload requires it, expect more.

But if you can get them home early or grant them a day off because they made the extra effort, reward them appropriately, and they will willingly do it all over again when you most need them to.

Team members frequently jump at the chance to choose salary over an hourly rate. Other than the kudos that comes with boasting to Mom and Dad that they're making sixty thousand dollars a year, team members can budget themselves with a sense of security. Nothing says loan approval better than the stability of a regular income.

Simple. Cost effective. Value for money. So why not just make everyone salaried?

Like so many things in life that are often too good to be true, there are exceptions and hurdles to this too. Whereas you can schedule a salaried exempt team member to work as you need, you cannot penalize them or take away a dime if they miss work, come in late, or fail to work outside their job description. Four weeks of jury duty or deployed to serve our country? They are entitled to get paid. A bad case of influenza? They get paid. Short work week thanks to three feet of snow and the business being closed? They get paid.

The definition of *salaried* also falls within the Fair Labor Standards Act for how you classify your team members. The Department of Labor determines that to be overtime exempt, the salaried team member must fall into one of three categories. So, be careful.

Let me share the best way to weigh the odds of whether you're playing within the rules before Sally gets her salary.

First is the executive exemption. If the salaried team member makes strategic business decisions—without requiring your approval—they will likely qualify. As an example, if without checking in with you first, they can determine prices for services, forgive a late payment, hire, terminate, and/or supervise other team members, you're good.

Second is the professional exemption where the primary duty of work requires skills that are acquired by prolonged, specialized fields. Think of teachers, engineers, doctors, and those with strong academic backgrounds. They qualify. A claim that your manager spent years at college, has a master's degree, and oversees the payroll of six team members but needs your signature to correct an error will not qualify them as exempt.

Third, and likely the most used, is the administrative exemption. To qualify, your candidate must have duties that include office or nonmanual work that supports the daily and long-term goals of the business. Again, they must have the *genuine* ability to use their discretion and judgment with what can best be described as serious issues and decisions. As an example, you might give this leader the authority to make or interpret policies; change a vendor; or independently review, promote, or give a pay increase.

If after reading this, you can look in the mirror with a straight face and reassure your reflection that your team member qualifies as exempt, go ahead. Remember the cautionary rule here for anyone salaried who doesn't fall into one of the categories above. If they work even one hour over forty in any given week, you *must*—by law—pay them overtime. Why? Because they are not salaried exempt. They are salaried nonexempt.

What baffles me is the arrogance of major US employers who have the benefit of highly paid—and salaried—human resources leaders and counsel and still violate the rules when they have no case for claiming ignorance. In court, your opposing counsel will accuse you of deliberately cheating your team members, with team member–friendly judges referring to it as "wage theft."

Walmart found out the hard way after being caught classifying managers incorrectly. With penalties, back pay, and damages, they paid out $5.3 million, which pales in comparison to Chipotle's $15 million payout, Humana's $17 million, or McDonald's being forced to write a supersized check for $26 million. Add Jimmy John's at $1.8 million and a Panera franchisee at $4.6 million and you can appreciate how dangerous a violation could be to your financial health. Don't be fooled by the size of these companies and think you're unlikely to get caught. The guy down the street shoots his neighbor, and it only hits the local news. A celebrity has a car wreck, and it becomes headline news. Only the ugly stories become famous, but it only takes a single phone call from a team member who feels cheated to experience the wrath of the Department of Labor. And rightfully so.

One last thought. If your manager is smart enough to be salaried, they can probably do simple math without your help. Don't lose a great team member because they figured out that the sixty thousand dollars you pay them for fifty-five hours a week is equal to less than twenty-two dollars an hour. Follow your heart and not your wallet on this one, and do the right thing.

> *You cannot push anyone up a ladder unless he be willing to climb a little himself.*
> **—ANDREW CARNEGIE**

This quote from Andrew Carnegie, an American industrialist and major philanthropist of the nineteenth century, speaks strongly to the fact that no matter how strong a leader is, they cannot push someone to success if that person is not willing to put forth the effort of climbing the ladder to success on their own.

CHAPTER 9

HANDBOOKS

---

hand·book

/ˈhan(d)ˌbook/

a book capable of being a ready reference

Every one of us, at one time or another, has picked up a book, eager to see where the story takes us, only to grow disappointed when we find ourselves bored before the first chapter is even over. The book is closed, never to be opened again.

The same applies to team member handbooks. They can be the most boring, uninspiring, self-defeating, and poorly written documents in the workplace. Frequently, well-intentioned writers lay the groundwork for potential lawsuits just by the way a handbook is written. But you have an obligation to set a motivational tone that reeks of your desired culture, because culture drives behavior.

One on one, I could give you dozens of examples of handbook entries that are simply diabolical and have no value whatsoever. Worse, they are a lawsuit waiting to happen. Avoid telling people what you won't tolerate and exchange your demands with what you love and look for. I hesitate to add this story and hope that the business owner who had this in their onboarding document as a warning for team members doesn't see it: "We don't like crybabies or drama queens." I understood what was being said and why it was being said, but you just simply can't say things like that.

Over the years, I have encountered everything from a three- or four-page handbook to a ninety-five-page (what should have been leatherbound) edition to a handbook that is more than five or six years old. Laws and times change, and so does the need for updated policies, procedures, guidance, and relevant content.

If there was one piece of advice I would give anyone about to embark on writing a handbook, it would be to think about the tone. What message or messages are you trying to convey to your target audience? How do you want to perfectly communicate the culture of your company, the style of your leadership, your core values, and the expectations you have for team members?

I think many writers who are tasked with this critically important piece of work believe that their job is to share everything a team member cannot do and the hundred reasons how and why they can be separated from the company. The alternative, and it's a lousy one, is to have a legally minded third party write it. There is so much focus on protecting the employer and creating legally sound landmines for what will happen if a team member fails that there is no consideration of the fact that the handbook should inspire, motivate, and retain the best talent. Not to share how many ways you can legally separate.

First, let's start by setting that tone. This can be accomplished by introducing, in less than a full page, the owners or senior leaders of your organization and mini bios, if you would like. Talk about how the company started, its grass roots, why you created it, what your goals are, what you hope the future holds, and then, most importantly, how pleased you are that your new team member has taken a leap of faith to join you and become a part of everyone's success. Alternatively, write a welcoming letter-style message as the opening, and add a copy of your personal signature.

Tone includes ensuring that the reader understands and genuinely believes in your commitment to an open-door policy where their ideas and/or complaints are welcomed. I like to think my door was always open to anybody who could follow the three *C*s when they had a complaint: be courteous, concise, and constructive. It's a nicer way of saying don't come into my office, be rude to me, repeat your grievance over forty minutes, and request the impossible.

Step two: Outline your core values and/or your mission statement in simple terms. Don't add explanations to either within the handbook. This should be shared during the onboarding process when you speak with your new team member. Share with passion what your core values are and why they are critical to you and everyone who is a part of the team.

Continuing with the importance of the tone, spend less time talking about how certain actions and behaviors can get team members into hot water and instead share how top performers are successful and how they are rewarded. I think it's okay to add a line to your handbook that says "Those who don't live by our core values will not be successful with our company," but at the same time, it's so much more positive to read a line that shares how much you appreciate flexibility, timeliness, and the ability to work well with others. Doesn't that read better than statements such as everyone must work when needed, be on time, and remain friendly and professional toward others? Same message; completely different tone.

Employers love to give themselves pages and pages of space so they can list all the infractions that can lead to separation. Frequently throughout handbooks is the word *discipline*. "Subject to disciplinary action up to and including a suspension or termination" is a human resource favorite and shows up throughout nearly every handbook I've ever read. Instead, state that an infraction may result in one or more opportunities to coach the team member. You can go as far as to say "coaching up to and including separation." Again, I want to share the difference in tone when you compare that to "Violations of this policy will result in disciplinary action up to and including termination." If your goal is to intimidate your new team member and be viewed as the scary boss, go right ahead, but I would highly recommend the *same message with a different tone*!

Going back to the list of a hundred things you can do wrong that will result in a team member's unceremonious departure, try reducing that number to as few as possible. Reason being, if you have someone who claims unfair dismissal or discrimination, my expectation is that the opposing attorney will ask you four questions during your endless and uncomfortable deposition. Number one: "You have a list of a hundred behaviors or policies that my client must abide by. Could you tell me exactly what those one hundred are without referring to the handbook, please?" Realizing that you cannot possibly remember all one hundred, the opposing counsel will continue with question number two: "Am I to understand that you cannot recall all one hundred but expect my client and each of your team members to remember them?" Number three is a doozy: "Of those one hundred infractions, how many did my client break in the five years they worked for you?" Counsel will continue to grill you. "Murder, manslaughter, and setting the building on fire aren't listed in your list. Am I to understand that by not adding those behaviors, they are acceptable?" I will guarantee you can't answer those questions with ease. "Finally, may I ask where within your list of one hundred infractions does the reason you terminated my client fall? In other words, which is the most important, and are they ranked by importance?"

This is a pure case of "less is more" and the reason I am totally committed to a professionally written set of all-encompassing core values that lay out pretty much everything you expect from a good team member. One last point to hammer home is this: if you are asking yourself whether you should or shouldn't add policy into your handbook, remember that there isn't a handbook in the world that tells team members they shouldn't turn up to work naked or spit on a customer. Rely on common sense wherever you can.

Now let me contradict myself completely for good measure. You absolutely should have policies that address "zero tolerance" and are critical to the health and safety of your team members, company, customers, vendors, visitors, and anyone else your team members may interact with. Excellent examples of this include substance abuse, bullying, harassment of any kind, and weapons in the workplace, etc.

If you have any policy that is subject to change within the next year or two, such as a vacation policy, bonuses, or any type of benefits, do not add it to your handbook; otherwise, you will have to rewrite it sooner rather than you might want. Instead, refer to the policy and state your position, such as that your company supports a robust benefits program that is outlined in a separate policy issued during the onboarding process.

> **Rely on common sense wherever you can.**

To be completely safe, you should read and review your own handbook at least once a year to ensure it is legally compliant, appropriate, and current. If you want to take an additional step in caution, either review it with your team members every couple of years or, more appropriately, revise and update it before reissuing, and take time to ensure everyone understands the reasoning behind the refreshed contents. It will be a good use of your time, instead of being challenged when someone tries to file a trivial lawsuit against you based on an outdated handbook.

Finally, whenever you do add to your handbook, please make it as objective as possible. Two leaders once wanted to add a policy that read "fingernails must be a reasonable length." We debated back and forth for quite a while as I tried to explain that what is reasonable to one is unreasonable to another. The same discussion involved (and frequently does in handbooks) hairstyles, hair color, length of skirts, the tightness of shirts, what exactly is meant by *stubble*, and the amount of jewelry considered excessive. A word of caution here: current laws address discrimination and work against any employer who restricts hairstyles that keep with the heritage, gender, and race, etc. of a team member. Going back to being objective, be as specific as you possibly can, but have an open mind to changing fashions and what is considered acceptable, not just by you but by your clients and team members too. Tattoos and piercings are a perfect example of how times have changed. We now see people in positions of leadership who sport several piercings and/or tattoos. Whatever you decide, don't make any decision to hire, transfer, or promote that is inconsistent with a policy in your handbook.

In order to build a rewarding employee experience, you need to understand what matters most to your people.
—JULIE BEVACQUA

Team member recognition is vital to engagement and success, but this HR quote by Rise People's chief revenue officer, Julie Bevacqua, indicates the significance of understanding what makes your workers tick.

If you want to develop a healthier business culture and work setting, you must ask team members directly about their wants and needs.

Keep an open exchange of ideas with each individual about their professional goals, and make them feel heard and valued, which in turn will keep them motivated for the long term.

CHAPTER 10

REWARDS AND BENEFITS

re·ward

/rə'wôrd/

given in recognition of one's service, effort, or achievement

For too many years, the concept of rewarding team members was limited to the basics. Vacation days and an annual bonus with the added promise of an annual review that could or could not include a nominal pay increase.

Today's workforce is different, and the need to create rewards and benefits has changed. We've moved from creating programs that improve retention to planning attractions that catch the eye of candidates.

Fast food restaurants, big-box retailers, and nonunionized companies have come to realize that they must reward hard work, longevity, and skills. The rising cost of healthcare benefits has been increasingly burdensome, and employers have been forced to find other ways to compensate.

Whether you're a fan or not, the Affordable Care Act and a younger workforce have helped. Access to healthcare has become more mainstream and moderately less important to the generations entering the workplace.

That leaves retention, which is where the need for creativity really comes into play. Earning a week of vacation after a full year of service and an impersonal check simply miss the mark. Meanwhile, 401(k) plans hold a much higher appeal to baby boomer and Generation X applicants. Nothing changes, however, for younger generations who are still far removed from retirement years. I constantly remind employers that millennials saw the devastation of the Great Recession as their parents lost their jobs, savings, and homes. They don't trust the system and truly live for today.

To retain today's team member, rewards need to be frequent and personal. Added dollars to a paycheck in the form of bonuses have limited value. The recipient might be grateful for a moment or two but will cynically view the taxes they paid and look at what's left with not much more than a shrug. In the several years I worked in the casino industry, the bonuses I earned were frequently six figures, and in one case exceeded my annual salary. I wasn't ungrateful, quite the contrary, but I felt cheated when I saw how much had been taken from my reward by the local, state, and federal governments. There's no blame on the employer here. But the sense of gratitude was slightly spoiled, and I'm convinced that more could be accomplished for less. If you are rewarding excellence or providing bonus compensation, consider grossing up the amount and issuing it in a separate check. A $250 check will help a team member in Missouri walk away with about $160 if they file as head of household. I would advocate for an added $50 for the team member with the $200 check, or two crisp one-hundred-dollar bills. Showing the taxes have been taken care of has a value much larger than the extra cost.

TIME FOR TEA!

To retain today's team member, rewards don't need to be tied to the almighty dollar. They **do** need to be frequent and personal.

Can I stress this one enough?

I've talked about the similarities of today's workers and their relationships with employers to the interaction and need for attention between children and their parents. My advice is simple. Exchange cash for time. Quality time.

That can mean a simple thank-you. An event where you are present or simply having fun is more valuable than some addition to the paycheck, regardless of size, unless it's enough to be truly life changing.

Team members are looking for a connection. As in any relationship, connection is the quality that really matters. Think about it this way. How many times do children say they would rather spend an hour with their parents than get an extra allowance? They may not say this in the moment, that's for sure, but there will come a time when they look back and think about the things they did and the places they went with their parents versus how much they were given financially.

The most fun I've had with my leadership team was while playing the six-foot tall Jenga game I mentioned earlier anytime we onboarded new staff. I saw it as such a great and genuine opportunity to make a first and lasting impression of who we really were. This is such a great example because instead of the Jenga game, I could simply have given everybody ten dollars, but what would have been the fun in that and how long would the memory have lasted?

Gift cards with a personal note work. They show you took time and remember your team members' names. Personalize the message, and you double the value. Hand deliver it or send it via mail versus leaving it on their desk, and you triple the value. On birthdays, avoid the breakroom store-bought sheet cake—unless you love the 1960s. Instead, have fun with ideas that are personalized. Find out what your team members like. Not everyone likes the hoopla of being called out. For some, a warm handshake and a handwritten birthday card with a gift card to a favorite store is key. For your outgoing personalities, cupcakes with their initials and their favorite flavored icing will win you mega-leader points. Does it take extra effort? Yes. Does your team see that you took the extra effort? Yes.

For team building, organize a fun quiz or office scavenger hunt. Take your team on a picnic, have everyone participate in a themed potluck to celebrate Halloween, or take everyone to a game. It builds trust and a genuine connection. There are hundreds of ideas on the web, but one of my favorites is called Spaghetti Tower Challenge. Break your team into smaller groups, if you're able, and give each group thirty pieces of uncooked spaghetti, a yard of masking tape, a yard of string, three marshmallows, a pair of scissors, and ten minutes. Their goal is to build the tallest tower with a marshmallow on top. Add to the fun by participating alone or with another leader. Whether you win or not, the results are the same. You have spent quality time with your team, humanized yourself, and had some fun. It shouldn't be lost on you that I don't talk about prizes here. Bragging rights are free. The only downside is clearing up the mess afterward and the ugly sight of a still-standing spaghetti tower six months later. Whatever you do … don't touch it!

These are all opportunities to help you be seen as more than just a boss or manager but as a leader who is human first and is keen to invest *time* in their team.

> On birthdays, avoid the breakroom store-bought sheet cake— unless you love the 1960s.

There are many ways to reward team members. I hesitate when recognition and reward are equal for everyone when the performance, loyalty, and hard work of every individual is different. With rewards like holiday parties, day trips, cash, or anything of value, it is hard to differentiate *fairly* and *equally*. Simply embrace that what you do for one, you must do for all.

Bonuses can be a complete waste of money, and then in other instances they can be extremely important and rewarding for both team members and the company. A good example of a what a complete waste of money looks like is bonusing a team member just for doing the job. Trust me—you won't get anything extra for your money. And if you are bonusing the team, remember this: the ones who work the hardest for you and give it their all earn the same as those who don't. How is that fair? Now all you have done is spend money to kill morale for your best team members while rewarding and wasting money on those who didn't earn it.

I am a proponent of losing bonuses altogether, except for those who are in sales and should be incentivized based on production. My preference is to think differently, and in this competitive world, rewarding team members is worth it. Pay a better wage and make increases worth earning. What I like to call my Fair Wage Program is very simple. For instance, instead of paying twenty dollars an hour and constantly advertising, I would much rather pay the same position twenty-three dollars an hour, attract a higher quality candidate from an increased pool of applicants, and set my standards and expectations higher. I also believe that annual increases, which are also a form of reward, should be impactful and a genuine incentive for high performance. Most recently, I inherited a system that included 1 percent and 3 percent increases for each yearly review. Think about the damage that can be done by that system. With team members earning as little as sixteen dollars an hour and being "rewarded" a 1 percent increase, which is worth about $250 a year after taxes, we were asking our leaders to motivate and encourage low performers to up their game and stay with us for another year. It was a brilliant way to suck the life out of the room for both parties.

We replaced the paltry raises with increases that were worth earning. Here, I stress the word "earning." Another year of service or a performance that meets expectations should not expect or earn an increase. Instead, those who exceed goals, set an example for others, are top performers, and are irreplaceable should be celebrated with personal and memorable reviews. As I mention in the "Reviews" chapter, reviews should align with your team members' work anniversaries, and you should think of them as your team member's employment birthday. Our increases for a frontline hourly team member are a minimum of fifty cents, but we make efforts to help them earn an extra seventy-five cents or one dollar an hour. Only by making increases impactful can they have any value. Now, our top performers move up, and our leaders congratulate them when they share that their increase has a value of over $2,000 a year. You haven't just motivated the team member; you've motivated the leader to do the same for others. The value of this change in our compensation is profound: increased morale, increased retention, and an increase in referrals from people who want to join us. This is magic in the making.

For benefits, employers can have some fun and get creative. Before I share ideas on how to differentiate yourself as an employer, let me share what I think must change.

An allotment of sick days has always seemed odd to me. Providing a set number of days that we permit team members to be sick without penalty leads to two unavoidable truths. Team members will use the days, regardless. It's impossible to believe that an entire team of people can be sick the same number of days each year. The other danger, of course, is the potential for someone to come in and infect others with a communicable disease, virus, or worse. What a joy it is to work alongside someone close to hacking up a lung or sneezing on everything within sight. Don't you want them to stay home?

Instead, reward your team members with a preset number of "no fault" personal time off (PTO) days from day one. Determine what you can afford and let your team bank the days to use them whenever they want—with reasonable notice if it's not for sickness. When I say "sick," that includes "sick of working." We must accept there will be days team members won't want to get out of bed and days they'll dread the idea of even getting showered or dressed. Don't fight it—welcome it. Let them stay home. If they came in, their productivity would be 50 percent of what you need, or worse. The value is in keeping them home to recharge, helping them feel guilt-free, and making it so they can return the next day ready to work. That's a win-win situation you shouldn't lose sight of.

A team member who tells you they didn't want to get out of bed is really telling you they lacked the drive to come to work. I need team members who, like me, wake up and are ready to see what's in store at work. Said once, it's fine; twice, it's worrisome; and three times, it's a clear sign. Question them, with respect, and see what's driving that comment. It's unfair to expect everyone to "want to work here." I don't think so.

I also recommend minimizing verbiage to the effect of "use them or lose them" in your policies. Trust me. As soon as they realize that rule exists, they'll use them—and probably at your busiest, most inconvenient times. It is acceptable, however, to limit the number of hours or days you permit a team member to carryover vacation or PTO. Be reasonable but not punitive. The risk of allowing unlimited carryover time could be receiving a resignation from a team member who has banked a few days every year for the past twenty years and is eligible for a huge payout. Earned? Yes. But if they saved three days from twenty years ago, the value of those hours will have changed if they entered the workforce as a twelve-dollar-an-hour team member versus their current salary of $83,200, equivalent to forty dollars hourly.

Other benefits can be inexpensive and also impactful. For instance, there are certain holidays team members expect. In the US, we expect—as right-of-passage—to be either off the schedule or paid extra for working on Independence Day, Thanksgiving Day, Christmas, and New Year's Day, at the very minimum. Most employers have up to six or seven days, with Easter, Memorial, and Labor Day factored in. But does Gen Y really understand or care about Memorial or Labor Day? They should, but do they? We now promote our positions with a list of benefits that include an added holiday: "Never Work on Your Birthday Again." It's designed, along with the rest of our efforts, to support our commitment to caring about our team members and letting them celebrate one of the most important days of their year. If their special day falls on a weekend or regular day off, they can use any day within the week prior to or after their birthday. Best of all, it's a one-size-fits-all benefit—everyone has one!

For employers who can accommodate flexible, remote work there are standout positives and negatives. The upside is a happier team member who can enjoy the flexibility of their schedule, focusing on the quantity and quality of their work from the comfort of their home, perhaps loving the new dress code that includes pajamas and no need to retrieve their car from the garage. For the employer, the benefits show in the slowdown of turnover, timely work, and a clearly happier teammate. Conversely, the negatives might include someone working from home, alone, with no direct supervision or mental stimulus from interacting in person with others. Employers will wonder if productivity might be hindered by personal interruptions or the ability of anyone to manipulate their hours on the job. However, if this is what team members of today are seeking or need, my advice to you is to meet that need. We go out of our way to meet the needs of our customers and clients. The time has come to do the same for our team members. Remember, the goal is to maximize the profitability of everyone on the team. If you *can* do it, do it. Use this motto: We always try to find ways to say *yes* versus no. An average school day in the US starts at 8:00 a.m. and finishes at 3:00 p.m. Appealing to moms who cannot get to work until 8:30 a.m. or need to leave at 2:30 p.m. could help fill several open positions. If you can offer split shifts, part time, or only mornings or afternoons, think outside the box and make it work. As a reminder, those who don't work a full week are more likely to turn up, take less time off, and may not need *all* the benefits afforded to full-time team members. Get ready, though: I'm about to contradict myself.

> *Keep your team satisfied by making sure they have great reasons to show up for work in the morning.*
> **—SHEP HYKEN**

That's a good segue into the topic of how part-time team members are treated. It irritates me when leaders joyfully mention that part-timers don't get any of the perks. "Yup … hired Mary. I made it so that she works only twenty-nine hours, can't earn PTO, doesn't get paid for holidays, and isn't entitled to …" Translated, what I hear is "I just hired someone I can cheat out of anything that will keep them here." You must pay them equally and might have to prorate the PTO and bonuses, but why wouldn't you treat them well? They should be giving you the same value per hour as your full-time team members, so reward them equally.

Creating benefits that are valuable in the eyes of your team members isn't always easy. Obviously you must remain profitable, so the idea of everyone getting a company car with an on-call chauffeur is likely out of the question. Set the stage by explaining what the goals are—retention and job satisfaction—and SOAR (support, opportunity, appreciation, and respect). I don't know that you need to explain that cost is a consideration. These aren't children who will ask for the moon. Nobody is going to suggest an all-expense-paid trip to Disney World. You can offer guidelines, such as not being able to close down for a whole day, not negatively affecting customer service, and making sure you're equitable to everyone, then let them get back to you with three or four ideas for your consideration. If you've explained the goals and guidelines clearly, the likelihood of finding something that is impactful is high. Remember, however, that this is about them and not you. Secondly, you might want to do the same exercise next year to keep it fresh and top of mind that you *care*.

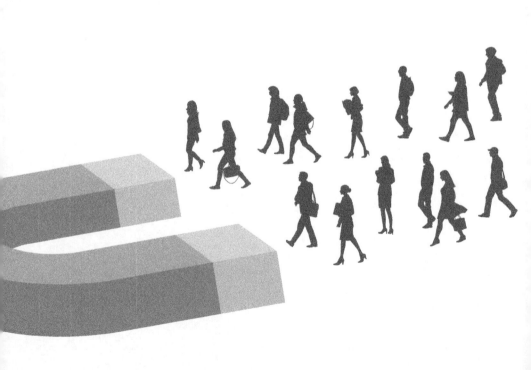

CHAPTER 11

MORALE KILLERS AND BOOSTERS

mo·rale

/məˈral/

the confidence, enthusiasm, and discipline of a person or group

The opportunities to kill morale are endless. Most troublesome to any leader is the realization that team members can be offended by a well-meant but badly received memo, comment, email, or meeting. Not easy, but there's true value in reading your room and checking yourself to see if you're directing your comments to one or two people you know have your back and will understand your good intentions. Consider for a moment that the meeting is going well. Those you know well are thinking the same thing. They're smiling and rather proud of their clear alliance with the leader. On the other hand, there are a few or more sitting there disillusioned, unclear on the vision, and feeling like they are the only people in the room who feel this way. They will leave that meeting with their morale seriously damaged.

I was once told by our vice president of gaming that I was regularly murdering the morale of our team. Respectfully, but firmly, she told me I had a habit of pointing out flaws of a few of our executives to everyone. Using the phrase "pepper-spraying the room," she described how top performers who were not guilty of the reprimand felt badly, leaving the room with their morale severely damaged. Way to go, Sean. "Instead," she suggested, "why not pull the offenders to one side and coach them?" Looking back, I think it was a combination of assuming that those I was addressing would understand my comment was directed at them and practicing a bit of cowardice on my part. I never made the same mistake again.

> *Children are accustomed to a continual stream of criticism and praise, but adults can go weeks without a compliment while enduring criticism both at work and at home. Adults are starved for a kind word. When you understand the power of honest praise (as opposed to flattery and sucking up), you realize that withholding it borders on immoral. If you see something that impresses you, a decent respect to humanity insists you voice your praise.*
>
> **—SCOTT ADAMS**

TIME FOR TEA!

Don't waste time looking back. You'll be distracted by the mistakes you've made instead of maximizing what the future holds.

Writing business plans can be an absolute nightmare, but companies insist their leadership teams produce these with a three-year vision for goals and the steps that will be taken to meet those goals. A company I worked for several years ago was led by good people who suffered from the impolite and disrespectful nickname "the seagulls." The first time I heard it, I asked a vice president to share what "the seagulls" meant. He paused before responding "We love them, but they have a habit of flying in from the corporate office, pooping on everything, and flying back out." One of these fly-in visits was to go through our three-year business plan. Despite a belief in their good intentions, I noticed they debated the contents for the afternoon and then left. We, in turn (given we weren't psychic and couldn't plan for an unknown recession, COVID, mass unemployment, or the city tearing up a main route to our front doors), put forth our best efforts. As soon as they left, we put the latest version of the business plan on a shelf and allowed it to collect an appropriate amount of dust before it was replaced the following year. It was a morale killer, and I hated leading the challenge with my team just as much as they hated participating in it. It took me a few years before convincing our corporate team to limit the business plan to just the following twelve months and, more importantly, to meet with us regularly to assess our progress and offer support where we might be missing goals.

Nobody enjoys being fed the new marketing plan, policies, or procedures. There are two camps in the world of leadership: those who make decisions and prefer to do so alone and those who make decisions based on the feedback of others. An executive and I went toe to toe over a new marketing plan for television, radio, and collateral. I asked who he had looked to for input. He literally went ballistic. "I have been in marketing my whole career, and I don't have the time to get everyone's opinion." Equal in position, I swore that the process of working alone would never apply. Why would you spring something major on your team without getting some input? In the case of uniforms or marketing, pick your top three choices, share them with a minimum of four people you trust who will give you candid feedback, and explain—without showing any bias—why each made your list. Avoid sharing your favorite, ask them to speak to why they picked one over the others, and restrict them to just one choice. You have the advantage of turning what could be a morale killer into a morale booster. You have created a *we* decision, where success or failure is shared. Experience tells me that your successes will outweigh your failures by a wide percentage.

According to a 2021 survey by Gartner, team members are naturally suspicious of any survey you might ask them to participate in, especially large groups of maybe fifty or more. The outcomes of a survey are usually predictable. When the results are not in their favor, people will always believe your survey was rigged. I've seen firsthand how the minority will openly declare they know everyone voted for choices *B* or *C* and certainly not the winning choice. Without a doubt, you will hear rumblings like, "I don't know why they ask for our opinion. They do what they want to anyway." If there is a solution, it would be to select six to ten team members with different levels of seniority or tenure and have them make the choice. Be careful not to pick your favorites or anyone who might be perceived as your favorite. In fact, this is an excellent opportunity for you to pick people who are not your fans, gain their support, and earn some confidence along the way.

Let's move on to a few ideas that can help boost morale no matter how small or large your team or business. Communication is a topic that comes up in meetings and exit interviews. You simply cannot overcommunicate with your team. I've been known to send out an inordinate number of memos. Despite having a reputation for issuing so many messages, I don't know that that has ever deterred me, because I want to ensure no one could ever claim they are always the last to know things. Leaders who work for you have an absolute obligation to make sure anything you send out is posted in a conspicuous area where everybody can read it. And if there are small meetings or morning huddles, they should be taking the opportunity to share the information and dialogue openly to avoid confusion or misinterpretation.

> You simply cannot overcommunicate with your team.

Understanding that every team member is different and has their own sets of priorities, loyalties, goals, and self-interests is a good reminder of how to keep morale high. In case you're interested, credit is given to Abbot Bernard of Clairvaux who apparently first coined the phrase "The road to hell is paved with good intentions." How many times have you heard a leader say "I treat everyone the same. In my mind, everyone is equal." We must accept that people are different and that the team is made up of several talents and varying levels of ability, dedication, and loyalty. I get a kick out of leaders who say "I just don't understand this generation. It's so different from mine." I will look whoever says this straight in the eye and respond: "Guess what, they don't understand you either!" Often adding "Don't you think our parents said exactly the same about us and our grandparents exactly the same about our parents?" Keep morale high by treating everyone as an individual and speaking to each with respect regardless of age, experience, or tenure.

In the same vein, a colleague of mine constantly builds team confidence and morale by occasionally turning up with Starbucks. He remembers who likes sugar or sweetener, skim milk, or half and half. His focus is not simply finding ways to treat people well but just going the extra mile. It doesn't have to be every week. It doesn't have to be every month. Instead, the gesture works so well when it's random and for no reason at all. He's reinforcing an excellent culture and maintaining team member morale simply by remembering everyone's personal taste.

A wonderful way to boost morale or maintain it is to show your team that you are a human being. Reinforce that you are not better, in any sense of the word, than them. Do this by openly admitting your mistakes, praising someone publicly, catching your own errors, and doing something as easy as sharing a lunch break with your team. Conversation should never include sex, religion, or politics, of course. But it can include a television show you've recently watched, a movie you would recommend, or a restaurant you want to try and would like opinions on. Don't force a conversation. Let others take the lead. Just join in and enjoy the camaraderie that comes from "breaking bread" together.

In closing, I'll admit this. I have been called out for my stand that team members are *not* family. Too many leaders and business owners love to think of them as family. At the risk of offending someone, I firmly believe the word *family* should be removed from any component of public communication in the form of handbooks, press releases, etc. My reasoning is simple. Family is someone who is by your side when a child is born; they're next to you when a loved one is on their deathbed; they will bail you out at 3:00 a.m.; they will go on vacation with you and listen as you share the most personal details of your life and marriage. Team members are not there when *family* is. There's another component that gets you in trouble with the word *family* when you are about to coach, suspend, or separate from a team member. You might hear things like, "They fired Susan after calling us family. Nobody in my family would have done that. She's been with us for nine years!"

What are they, then? Teammates. Team dynamics and memberships change at work just as they do in sports. The weakest player is often traded or shown the final red card. Avoiding the word *family* is prudent to not killing morale. Instead, use *team* and maintain positive morale.

I was walking into work at 6:00 a.m. one morning and upon my arrival was immediately questioned by two team members on why I had ordered the heat to be turned off at 2:00 a.m. I hadn't. Instead, I had encouraged our Director of Facilities to find ways to cut our power bill. "Take a look at dropping the hot water temperatures down a degree, perhaps add sensor lighting to offices and hallways where nobody works past 7:00 p.m., and maybe cut back on spaces we're unnecessarily heating."

Just suggestions that maybe should have been interpreted as recommendations, but there was no directive and certainly no mandate.

His fault? Absolutely not. Lesson learned.

TIME FOR TEA!

Team members, regardless of how well you train them, are not—unfortunately—mind readers.

In considering what you say, you must define what might be interpreted as a directive.

Is it a suggestion?

Is it a recommendation?

Is it a directive?

Is it a mandate?

Suggestions are nothing more than that, whereas a recommendation might be based on an experience from the past. A directive is what you would like done, although it still welcomes debate, whereas a mandate is not open for discussion.

CHAPTER 12

PROMOTIONS AND TEAMS THAT CHANGE

pro·mo·tion

/prə'mōSH(ə)n/

an activity that supports or provides active encouragement

change

/CHānj/

the act or instance of making or becoming different

There are so many reasons a team changes. One of your longest-serving team members, maybe even your best, decides to retire. Alternatively, a few more quit with little or no notice at around the same time. Maternity or paternity leave taken by a team member who plays a critical role in your organization can change the dynamics and even the culture of a group of people, large or small. Expansion of your business, onboarding someone new, or acquisition and sudden growth can have immediate positive or negative, long-term or short-lived effects on how everyone works together. Frequently, like a thief in the night, change can happen without forewarning. Everything eventually changes, like it or not. Change itself is usually the outcome of one or more dominant personalities or team members who possess a great deal of influence or responsibility, leaving your business temporarily or permanently impacted—or worse—becoming a negative influencer for the rest of your team. This is the perfect time to mention a great book I happily recommend to anyone in a leadership role. *The Energy Bus*, written brilliantly by Jon Gordon, speaks to the "energy vampires" you must avoid at all costs when hiring for your team. Change *can* make someone into an energy vampire overnight. I've experienced it firsthand, and it's unpleasant to see someone go from being a productive and positive worker to someone who is bitter, hurt, and hates every minute of work because they feel they have been forced into a new way of life they didn't ask for.

Change is inevitable in life. You can either resist it and potentially get run over by it, or you can choose to cooperate with it, adapt to it, and learn how to benefit from it. When you embrace change, you will begin to see it as an opportunity for growth.

—JACK CANFIELD

Let's start with the resignation of a tenured leader and the subsequent question of who will replace them once the announcement is made. There may be several choices or very few, and there's usually an expectation that regardless of whether somebody is qualified or not, you should always promote from within. As a business owner and company executive, I can tell you that's not always the best decision. But how will you share that perspective with the rest of your team and disappoint someone who genuinely believes that job could or should be theirs? That's a real challenge, and my advice is very simple: quickly determine the best decision, not for you personally and not for the team, but for your business. You are not in business to make friends, despite the appeal of keeping everyone happy. If the best decision is to find an outside candidate, you must take steps to protect yourself and the morale of everyone involved.

The first step includes posting the position internally with a clear outline of the job title and description of the duties and responsibilities. Avoid the temptation to include anything that relates to internal candidates versus external. The message you are sending should be clear: the position is open to all qualified candidates. Don't exaggerate or minimize your expectations for who will fill the position. Take the time to consider whether the person who is replacing your existing team member will have added or perhaps fewer responsibilities. Maybe you want them to work longer hours or different days. This is also your opportunity to revamp your organizational chart and/or the job description. Perhaps the senior-level position doesn't need to be filled or the duties and responsibilities of the position can be shared by one or more of your existing team members, providing you an opportunity to increase compensation and/or benefits.

I examine every change in staff as an opportunity to reset my chessboard and wherever possible—with the least disruption—make changes. Once again, however, those changes should benefit nothing else but the business and its long-term success.

When you post internally for the position, ensure you have three critical components of the posting:

- **Number One:** Make sure there is a deadline for candidate applications.

- **Number Two:** Ensure everyone has an opportunity to see the posting. Avoid a situation where you display the posting on the wall of the break room for a week while one of your team members is out of office, technically disqualifying them from applying. You can imagine the resulting fallout and perception from such a sloppy and thoughtless move.

- **Number Three:** Outline the decision-making process. Make it clear who will conduct interviews and who the position will report to. Do not allude to any time frame. By doing so, you will tie yourself down when it might take weeks or months to find the right fit for the role.

If a dominant or influential team member is on temporary leave due to maternity, jury duty, military, illness, or otherwise, you might also witness a change. Keep your eyes and ears open. There's a possibility the team might work better and more efficiently with each other and for your business. Perhaps the absence of one person proves to be beneficial and a surprisingly positive change occurs. That will leave you with the challenge of determining how to address the missing team member once they return. If you like the changes you've observed, be frank and candid. Share what you've seen and how you want the positive changes to become part of the business's future environment and culture. Leave no doubt in this individual's mind that you like what you see, and your expectation is that they will embrace the changes, which in turn will require a change in their style of leadership.

Alternatively, the missing team member could have a very detrimental effect on the staff's efficiency and teamwork during their absence. It's not unusual for team members to feel like abandoned ships in the night when their leader leaves, even for a short period of time. Perhaps they rely on this person too much? That leads to the question, What would I do if this person left? If the missing link will be gone for an extended period, you have some decisions to make. Do you temporarily put someone in that role, or do you take ownership and lead the team yourself, accepting the ensuing responsibilities? The same challenges occur when one or more team members leave either at the same time or for just a short period. Recognize how things are changing and determine what steps must be taken to glue your team together and ensure others don't jump ship; your clients, customers, patients, or guests, are not negatively affected; and your business doesn't suffer.

> *As I navigate my career, I recognize how things must and do constantly change. From business and personal goals, priorities, roles, team members, locations, finances, and more, it all combines into one moving target.*
>
> *There will always be another goal or obstacle to tackle, but there is a greater need to embrace change.*
>
> **—DR. SAM J BURROW IV, DMD, MS**

Several years ago, I was offered the position of vice president, joining two other professionals in the same role and reporting to the president. The job itself was exciting. My new role held me responsible for the oversight of marketing, food and beverage, human resources, security, and the business development of a multimillion-dollar revenue company with seven locations covering the US and the Caribbean. What made this an interesting but ultimately disastrous decision was complicated by three unique factors. The president was not only a former team member but had grown to be one of my closest friends who, quite frankly, went out of her way to create the position for me. She knew I needed a change and a fresh opportunity, and, in many ways, this was a perfect fit for my career based on prior experience and accomplishments. They say in movies, don't work with animals or children. The same could be said for business and working for friends. We worked tremendously well with each other, but there were other dynamics that got in the way, which led to my resignation less than a year after relocating to the corporate office. However, let me be very clear that to this day, she is one of the very best friends I have. It was the fault of no one that neither she nor I realized that the opportunity for success in such a dynamic would be slim. We couldn't have predicted what would happen.

TIME FOR TEA!

Don't put anyone on a pedestal who quickly becomes a statue.

It hurts everyone, including the person who is newly promoted.

One of my new corporate counterparts who had also been a former team member and was now my equal welcomed me with open arms. The second of what was now a team of three also did what she could to make me feel at home and integrate me into the culture and inner workings of the company. What we had missed, but was staring us right in the face, was the fact that the three of them, the president and two corporate vice presidents, had worked so professionally and intimately together for so many years that it was impossible to infiltrate their interpersonal and professional dynamics and make the changes I wanted to introduce. Together, they had so much history, knowledge, and a firm grip on the culture of the business that no matter what I did, could do, or wanted to do, I was always going to be the third wheel, and it was never going to work. Several years later, they remain hugely successful and any contribution I might have made will never really be known. But one thing I know for sure is that had I stayed, it would have changed the recipe that was already hard baked and, quite simply, worked for them. I gain a little satisfaction knowing that they never tried to replace that position, and I remain the first and last corporate vice president of brand and business development for that company.

I share this story to illustrate how one new team member can or cannot influence the company. As an owner or senior leader of any organization, it's your responsibility to do two things.

1. Make every effort possible to ensure that new team members are welcomed with open arms.

2. Stay alert for changes, good or bad, that their presence influences, especially with tenured team members.

Lastly, I want to share some insight on when you acquire another office or location for your business. Once you sign on the dotted line, you're pretty much getting a building, customers, and a brand, not to mention you're also essentially adopting a new team. What happens next comes down to you.

Over several years, I built a brand, starting with one location and ending up with many. During those years, I observed two distinct behavioral impacts to the teams, both old and new. I observe new people with caution and hesitancy, wondering if they will fit well with us and vice versa. And then there is what I refer to as my legacy team: those who were the first team members and the bedrock of our company.

As we grew, there were opportunities to improve many aspects of how we operated. Ideas from our original location were introduced to the new team, who were now a part of our company. At the same time, we were learning how to integrate some best practices of the business we had just purchased. What mattered most was not how good the ideas were but how we introduced them and made everyone feel part of one company versus two. It's easy for your original team to feel the new location is getting all the attention and love. On the contrary, the new team can, without a lot of care and attention, feel secondary. Watching from the sidelines while ultimately taking responsibility for how the teams integrate with each other is critical.

With the company growing from one location to the next, it was interesting and intriguing to see how we managed to become one cohesive company. Without a very clear commitment to a structured integration, I am convinced we would have failed. I was insistent that we blend ourselves into any acquisition we made instead of bulldozing our way in with ideas. It was incumbent upon us. With a commitment to retaining as many team members as possible and creating success of the business as well as we could, we had to learn what had made the business attractive enough for us to purchase it. At the same time, we had to remember it was those team members who in large part led to the business's success and, in turn, our decision to acquire it.

Individual commitment to a group effort— that is what makes a team work, a company work, a society work, a civilization work.

—VINCE LOMBARDI

So true, and the message is clear enough. Let's not forget, though, that to get the team working to their potential—however willing they are to produce excellent results together—there must be a vision, expectations, and a leader.

One aspect of acquisition that is often forgotten is the impending loss of the owner or manager that the acquired team was working for and the impact of that loss. Team members are similar, in some respects, to children who have lost a parent, watching from the sidelines as they are replaced by someone who has their own rules, habits, and idiosyncrasies. With changes in leadership, how many times have you heard "But that's not the way we've always done it!" Imagine what a culture shock it is when an owner disappears, sometimes suddenly.

I have always advocated that the seller and new owner should be seen together frequently during a transition. This communicates to everyone that the likelihood of happiness and continuity is possible, if not guaranteed. Trust is built when the "departing parents" and the "new parents" clearly get along.

The only exception is when the seller themselves is either disliked or distracted. During the transition period of an early salon acquisition (still part of my world to this day), I spent time with the seller who shared how he cheated his team members with salaries and vacation time. He was well known to be a penny-pinching, selfish, money-hungry person who cared little to nothing about his team members and only about the profits he could grab for himself. Although we had agreed upon a two-to-three-week transition period, it made perfect sense to tell him on my first day of ownership that it was his last day, and that I would be taking over completely and immediately without his help. The interpretation of what was about to occur was clear—him staying would have been a reflection on me, and I would be labeled as more or less the same. His team members knew exactly what he was about. How he had managed to keep so many of them for so many years remains a mystery to me. What I can say is that I am proud of how everyone on that original team has grown and is still with me today.

To sum it up, if you are about to acquire a company, be sensitive to the qualities of the person you are replacing. Do you want to emulate their leadership style, culture, and values, or do you want to go in a different direction completely? If so, be honest and just own it. Share your vision and invite them to join you in the journey. If you think previous leaders staying on has nothing to do with you, count the days before some or most of your team members quit on you. And before they leave, most will happily tell your clients or customers how little you know and how terrible the changes are, closing off with "Who knows what else they'll do!"

The secret is simple. Listen, learn, consider change; measure the effects of potential change; communicate the change; and then make the change. It's also important to stick to the change until it's proven to either work or fail. Never be afraid to backtrack, admit you failed or made a mistake, and rectify the change or changes.

Ultimately, the obligation of keeping a pulse on the change within an organization, company, business, or team is your responsibility! Leaders lose people when they are mentally asleep at the wheel with no idea that change is occurring, tides are shifting, and people are leaving. You can find out so much just by asking team members how things are. One last thought is to emphasize the importance of asking the quiet ones—those who never complain or ask for anything extra—because it is likely that they will leave you first, and you will be the last to know.

> *The more seriously you take your growth, the more seriously your people will take you.*
> **—JOHN MAXWELL**

This quote comes from an American author and motivational speaker who believes that a company cannot succeed without its leaders succeeding first.

Team members want to see their leader putting in just as much effort into their success as they do. A leader who takes their own growth seriously and who adapts their methods to better suit their environment and progress toward success will be inspiring.

CHAPTER 13

SEPARATION

---

sep·a·ra·tion

/ˌsepəˈrāSH(ə)n/

the action or state of moving or being moved apart

Every word we use in the workplace, verbalized or written, reflects company culture. Words can be ugly and have a negative effect on morale and company reputation. Having said that, I would like to talk about *separation*. I don't like the words *fired* or *terminated*. If you use either of those, how do you differentiate saying goodbye to someone who gave their absolute best but didn't quite make it versus saying goodbye to a team member caught stealing from you?

When you say goodbye to someone after agreeing the position wasn't the right fit, nobody will understand it was a friendly parting if you use the word *fired* in a memo. The same connotation and misunderstanding occurs when you use the word *terminated*. Remember, be consistent with the words you use for every team member, in each distinct situation, if only to avoid accusations of favoritism or discrimination. Consistency is key.

Using the word *separation* shows a modicum of respect to the person you are bidding farewell, regardless of the circumstances. You might wonder, who cares if the thief who embezzled from me is "separated" from the company versus "fired"? The result is the same, I agree. However, I do care that the well-intentioned, ultimately ill-fitted team member who is moving on to other opportunities leaves as someone who separated and respects us and is being respected by us. Let me stress again: your team members are watching and reading into everything you do and say. Make sure they know you have a sense of decency and honor if a parting of ways is mutual and without ill will.

> *When the norm is decency, other virtues can thrive:*
> *integrity, honesty, compassion, kindness, and trust.*
> **—RAJA KRISHNAMOORTHI**

How you separate a team member is just as important as the words you use. After several successful and rewarding years as senior executive of a publicly owned company, I was told my services were no longer required by the company that had acquired us. How was I separated from the job I loved and the people I worked with? The answer is quite simple: with a total lack of respect and disregard for my feelings during what was a life-changing event. It did not matter that I was given a full year of severance pay and benefits. The person I was then reporting to appeared to lack any traces of human tact or kindness. He was full of himself and thoroughly enjoying his new executive powers. In his mind, as the "leader," there was a determination that it was quite appropriate to deliver this news over the phone while I was driving to work at 7:30 a.m. Being distracted by this bombshell, I'm surprised I wasn't pulled over for driving without due care and attention. I felt physically ill, not only because I had lost a position it had taken me forty years to attain but because of the degree of disrespect and callous disregard. How you say goodbye to someone is a reflection on your character and you as a person. Looking back, I think one of the most egregious aspects of that dreadful day was the insistence that I lie to my team. The classic "I've chosen to resign to pursue other opportunities" was demanded of me repeatedly before I was forced to face my team of directors and vice presidents. Years later, my father asked me, "Have you gotten over it?" I answered honestly and told him I never will. I was treated well and was paid handsomely to disappear, but the humiliation was brutal and the delivery was heartless. He made the right decision for himself and the company, I'm sure, but I would have traded the severance package (well, maybe not *all* of it) for some respect. That said, there was a humorous ending to our working relationship. Immediately after I followed his instructions and announced the fictional reason for my departure, he stopped by my office and told me I could work the rest of the week as I wanted and was free to come and go as I wished. Seriously? I had the keys to every lock, access to millions of dollars, the ability to wreak havoc wherever I wanted, and the responsibility of over $550,000 in revenue on an average day. Stay? I don't think so. To top it off, he offered, "If ever you're in the St. Louis area and you want to stop by for dinner, I'll pick up the tab. Just let me know." I didn't know how to react other than to say "I think the likelihood of that is pretty slim … but thank you."

But forget about me for a second and think about what his actions said to everybody else, not only in that conference room but to the 1,500+ team members who worked for me. What my executioner forgot was that my team members, specifically my direct reports, knew me and immediately knew who this new company was and how they operated. The ripple effect was instantaneous, and it was no longer about me; it was about them. Everybody, especially at and above the manager level, knew that tomorrow, it could be them. Good people were scared. Some started looking for new jobs and grew unfocused. It did not matter that I was one of many who was discarded, but it could and should have been handled in a way that showed compassion and respect. My hope is that by reading this story, you will remember the effect you have on people when it is time to say goodbye, regardless of why.

TIME FOR TEA!

You have nothing to lose and everything to gain by never making a decision to hire, promote, transfer, or separate a team member without a good night's sleep. "Maybe you'll feel differently in the morning" is sound advice. Allow yourself to find a different solution and minimize the chances that your decision isn't the best, or wake up and know for sure that you are doing the right thing **right**.

So how *do* you do it?

First, are you sure you want to say goodbye? This is a good rule of thumb I used: If a team member was being separated for theft, the *proven* use of illegal substances, physical harm to another person, or a loss of their state license, nobody could authorize the final decision without my knowledge and approval. As the most senior member of the team, I felt it was important every team member have the reassurance of a fair and impartial decision. Not only did this speak to our company culture, but it sent a message that we wouldn't tolerate favoritism or discrimination and allow someone to lose their livelihood just because their supervisor or manager disliked them or had a personal vendetta. This was a long way from our team members feeling like they might have a target on their back. Justification that could be substantiated was key before my signature found its way to the final entry in their personnel file.

If you want to avoid any form of legal action, whether by an attorney or the Equal Employment Opportunity Commission (EEOC), reassure yourself that sufficient, fair, and unbiased documentation exists. Without it, save yourself some time and go ahead and write a check—a big one. Unfair dismissals, regardless of who the victim is, how old they are, their race, sex, religion, or any other factor, can and will be awfully expensive. Wherever and whenever possible, allow a third party to review your decision. If an attorney specializing in labor law is unavailable, ask yourself this question: Is this the right decision, is it a fair decision, and is this going to come as a surprise to the person it affects?

> *How I wish we lived in a time when laws were not necessary to safeguard us from discrimination.*
> **—BARBRA STREISAND**

When you are separating the employment of a team member, think about what that person will tell their spouse, best friends, and family about why they lost their job. Think about how many people will actually tell the truth about why they do not work for you anymore.

When it's time to make that final decision, giving thought to how you'll conduct yourself is important and, again, a reflection on you and your leadership. It's good to have a "witness" during the meeting, but I am often shocked when two or more people join a leader for the conversation. I call that a firing squad. Not only is that intimidating, but it's also unnecessary, and the chances of gossip and speculation increase.

Key to the meeting is the setting. Make sure you find someplace you will be uninterrupted and that you have rehearsed exactly what to say. It is especially important to remind your witness that they are present as just that: a witness. Also inform them that the meeting is confidential and that they should not add to the conversation. They are there only to observe and listen. Also be clear that their role is to remain unbiased and that after the meeting, they should go straight to their office and document exactly what they saw and heard with loyalty only to the truth. Have them sign and date the document they create, and keep it securely in their possession, not yours. This can be a crucial piece of evidence and support for you later on, if you conducted the separation correctly.

My advice to anyone who must make these decisions is to always stick to the facts, speak calmly and clearly, and provide information about the following:

- Who to contact if the team member has questions

- How they can collect their personal belongings

- What will happen regarding their benefits, including information about COBRA, if applicable

- How and when you want company property to be returned

- And what questions they want you to address

Do not, under any circumstances, find yourself in a situation where there is debate, raised voices, or dispute. The decision has been made, and you should stick to it unless something remarkable is shared that would make you second-guess it, which in my experience has never happened. Do not apologize, and do not hug or cry, all of which I have witnessed and which displays company fault and guilt for the decision.

One last thing. Do the right thing and reassure your former team member that you will not allow for gossip, speculation, or disrespect regarding their separation. It is perfectly fair for you to share that you will announce this separation but that no further discussion or sharing will occur. Escort them out, allow them to collect personal belongings, but don't permit conversations with anybody. Depending on the circumstances, it is perfectly fine to shake hands, but I suspect that shaking your hand will be the last thing on their mind. Do as you promised and make the announcement either in person or via email, and keep it short. Remind everybody that a part of your culture includes respect for everyone and that discussions about the former team member will not be acceptable. All this will serve you well should you be sued by an attorney or charged by the Department of Labor for unfair dismissal.

It's also good to have a team member separation checklist to ensure you've taken all the necessary steps. Your list should include the following (and anything additional your organization or state may require):

- Either a separation letter or notice to the team member

- Whatever notices your state requires you provide to the team member

- Any severance pay the team member will receive put in a written agreement to be signed by both of you

- Written notice regarding the team member's health benefits and their rights to COBRA together with any flexible spending accounts accrued, etc.

- Written information regarding the team member's retirement plan

- A record of any moneys owed to the team member and how and when they can expect to receive their final paycheck

- Written noncompete agreements, if required

- The procedure for return of company property (i.e., cell phone, uniform, laptop, ID, company car, etc.)

- A document signed by the team member stating that they have removed their belongings from the property

- Disablement of the team member's access to any alarm system or online access, including voice mail and email logins

Having a separation checklist is vital to ensuring your separation is completed with integrity and legality.

Finally, I have two recommendations to add. The first is that if you are not 100 percent sure *that* all your ducks are in a row, get legal advice. It's not inexpensive, but it's a lot easier and less expensive than having to hire a defense attorney, sit through an eight-hour deposition justifying your decision, and then writing a settlement check. The second is to ensure you add a notation to the file: *Hire* or *No Rehire*.

If the team member reapplies after a few years, your memory may not serve right. But a quick look at the file will help you make the right decision.

> *There is great comfort and inspiration in the feeling of close human relationships and its bearing on our mutual fortunes—a powerful force, to overcome the "tough breaks" which are certain to come to most of us from time to time.*
> **—WALT DISNEY**

At the Walt Disney Company, team members and cast members make magic happen. Disney strives to create an optimal team member experience while meeting the business needs of the company.

CHAPTER 14

AMERICANS WITH DISABILITIES ACT

dis·a·bil·i·ty

/ˌdisəˈbilədē/

a physical or mental condition that limits a person's movement, senses or activities

A client calls and asks for help, challenged by the fear that their business is in jeopardy because of the Americans with Disabilities Act (ADA). A claim based on the client's refusal to buckle to an employees' demands was delivered in a letter from a renowned attorney. My client expected the worst outcome.

A team member with several years of service was claiming a mental disability for missed deadlines and an unreliable performance that was progressively getting worse. Close to retirement, the team member had a great deal of responsibility and wanted to stay in the same role, receive the same pay, do less, and have reduced accountability. The request was refused. She expected to be accommodated for her condition and backed it up with a letter from her physician confirming her claim.

The question was: Do we fight, and if we do what's the cost?

Let's be clear on what the ADA does and doesn't demand. As an employer, you are most definitely required to make a reasonable accommodation for any diagnosed disability. This would mean that for a manager who has severe back problems, you would need to accommodate a request for a chair with a supportive chair back.

It means that your front desk receptionist with carpel tunnel syndrome shouldn't be asked, or expected, to lift a full water jug into the cooler every time it runs dry. Each of those are what could and should be considered as reasonable accommodations. However, what the law doesn't require is accommodation of any need that is unreasonably burdensome to the business, will disrupt its long-term success, or will turn a blind eye to anyone who doesn't meet the requirements of the job itself. Here is what you do if a front desk receptionist, after six months on the job, tells you that because you don't have an elevator, it worsens their condition and demands you either allow them to work from home, install an elevator, or move your business from the second floor: you tell them a sympathetic *no*. The request is not reasonable in the eyes of the law. You are not expected to spend $125,000 on an elevator, move to a new address, or expect them to be a great front desk receptionist from home. There's one caveat to consider. If you were to have an open position, such as an accounts payable clerk, and the job could reasonably be completed remotely, I would err on the side of caution and make sure that the offer was theirs to either accept or refuse.

Let's return to the manager with crippling back pain. There is no protection for work that is riddled with errors or a week overdue.

Neither does it excuse a receptionist from taking notes for phone calls because it causes her pain. Reasonable accommodation expects fairness on both sides. You provide the chair and delegate the water cooler responsibilities to someone else, and in return they provide you with quality work and the established deadlines a job requires.

However, it's quite easy to lose your case if you don't play by the rules. You shouldn't double down and go to court and expect a good outcome. If time isn't on your side, and you don't have time for three or four depositions, you might determine that writing a check and settling is easier. Let's presume you just wanted the problem to go away, so a $25,000

> **Reasonable accommodation expects fairness on both sides.**

check to your former team member and another $25,000 for your attorney felt the easiest way to get back to business. In that case, let the negotiations begin.

Or you could avoid all that.

When challenged by clients who want to know if and how I could help, four questions come to mind, each usually accompanied by a regrettable moan. Let's start with the questions and follow up with the reasoning behind why they are collectively so important.

First. Do you have a clearly written handbook that covers progressive coaching?

Second. Does the team member have a clear and defined job description?

Third. What did the team member's last review or evaluation say?

Finally. How old are each of these documents, and are they in the personnel file with relevant signatures?

As your $750-plus-per-hour employment attorney preps you for the deposition, there will be time for you to practice how to respond to your former team member's pit bull counsel. Expect the proceedings to go something like this: "So, my client, who has worked devotedly for you for eighteen years, has never received so much as a verbal warning, has been given glowing reviews, and has received two promotions and fifteen pay increases is being asked to pull reports that aren't even on the job description you're presenting as evidence. To top it off, the job description doesn't have my client's signature, which tells me my client never saw it." As you try not to lose your mind, he will likely continue. "This is about the age and paygrade of my client and the fact that you can replace them with someone else to save yourself a lot of money." Suddenly, the claim changes from a violation of the Americans with Disabilities Act into a triple-threat EEOC hostile work environment, constructive dismissal, and an age discrimination case.

"After presenting you with a perfectly reasonable request for accommodation, you chose to refuse any notion of help and, instead, demanded the unreasonable."

Document everything. Immediately. Good, bad—it doesn't matter. A great way to avoid the taboo associated with "I got written up" is to flip the negative to a positive. Email your team member and recount the meeting you had in a positive manner.

Jenny,

Thank you for meeting with me to talk more about the need for excellent customer service. I appreciated the opportunity to share my concerns and how our tone of voice can make all the difference. I am confident that our next conversation will be positive, and I have every faith that you will be successful.

Sean

Press Send, but not before copying yourself and filing the correspondence someplace you'll easily recall.

As owners and business leaders, we create handbooks, job descriptions and reviews, but I can't unring the bell for you if you're not prepared. Avoid the unthinkable by getting your house in order. Today. The alternative is to write the check and try not to smudge the ink as you hand it over.

To handle yourself, use your head; to handle others, use your heart.
—ELEANOR ROOSEVELT

This quote is from the former first lady of the US and stresses the significance of compassion in great leadership. Being a good leader doesn't just mean you know how to assign roles and encourage company success. It means you also have the emotional intelligence necessary to pay attention to the needs and feelings of others and act appropriately in response to them. Excellent leaders know how to relate to their workers just as well as they know how to implement a course of action.

CHAPTER 15

HR FILES MADE SIMPLE

sim·ple

/ˈsimpəl/

plain, basic, or uncomplicated

Something important I've learned over the years is that no matter the nature of the business, owners just want to do the work they're trained for, practice the discipline they're an expert in, or enjoy their dream job. Dentists just want to take care of teeth, divorce attorneys simply want to handle what's in their clients' best interests, and retailers simply want to sell whatever is on the shelves. The idea of having to fill out paperwork, especially W-4s, I-9s and payroll deduction requests, is agonizing—especially when you know that the same set of forms must be completed for every new hire. To stay legally compliant, it's critical you fill out these forms in a timely manner and make sure they are complete and accurate. I have never joined a company or met a single client who has every personnel file in perfect shape. Much of the time, that is simply because it's time consuming and some of the forms themselves are ambiguous, and how you answer the questions can be confusing to even the most intelligent people. Because you're not an HR expert, you don't always know how to answer the questions a new team member has, such as what they should put for their deductions on a W-4? The I-9 form must be filled out within 3 days of employment to be considered valid. Certain documentation required by law cannot be outdated, go unsigned, or be incomplete. Personnel files may be checked to see if a federally required form should be stored separately from everything else.

TIME FOR TEA!

As a leader, you are not expected to welcome negative feedback with open arms, but you must welcome it with an open mind.

During a team member file audit I was completing for a client, I discovered paperwork that didn't belong and also documents that were missing. One team member who had been with the employer for over ten years had a personnel file that was at least three inches thick. Vacation request forms, sick notes, birthday cards, counseling notices, old reviews, and more are not only unnecessary but carry the risk of liability. A great piece of advice for any employer: Dispose of any written counseling that is more than a year old to avoid being accused of never forgetting a past sin. The same goes with reviews. Use last year's evaluation to recap and reference how you will review a team member for the current year. Once you have completed the new review, question whether there is value in keeping the old one. If you issue annual reviews, it's a good time to file clean and update relevant records. Don't forget to shred anything you dispose of versus trashing it. If you are ever challenged by an attorney or the Department of Labor about your document destruction for old reviews, your answer is valid and indisputable: "We review and focus only on the past year of performance and compare it to the previous year to see how our team members have met established goals." Going back further than a year is like trying to predict performance. Neither is relevant.

Employers frequently miss or don't understand that everything within a team member's file is subject to review by an opposing attorney. I'm not advocating that you destroy anything that should be maintained, such as a complaint from a team member, the results of an investigation, or documentation that is a record of action taken in defense of a team member or results in any form of counseling, suspension, or separation. If I had to choose a rule of thumb, it

> ## Going back further than a year is like trying to predict performance. Neither is relevant.

would be this: use common sense and ask yourself the question, Does this piece of paper have any value now or in the future? If you wouldn't want your team member to see it, or their attorney, it probably doesn't belong in the file unless it's covering up a poorly handled or negative result that affected you. This includes making personal notes that refer to a team member's performance, attitude, personal attributes, political views, religion, sexual preference, race, or anything that, quite frankly, is unjustifiable. A note that pertains to documentation that involves an investigation of any kind should be kept separate and confidential.

In team member files, I advocate for you to keep notes that are both dated and detailed and that will help you complete a thorough and accurate annual review when the time comes. Notes on a team member who goes above and beyond, is responsible for a positive social media review, or has an idea that increases your efficiency or profitability should be added to the file. At the same time, keep a record—dated and detailed—that will remind you about team members' infractions, such as tardiness, rudeness, violation of your core values/standards, or complaints from your customers or clients. These notes can be valuable during an annual review where it becomes clear to the team member that you have documented, by date, some of their most valuable contributions. Imagine sitting across from a team member and saying

> *"I rated you highly in the area of customer service, remembering that on April 5 you handled a very difficult situation with one of our customers who was making unreasonable demands and was quite rude."*

It doesn't take much to realize the positive effect memory can have. On the flipside, documenting every tardy or violation of any of your policies and procedures can be a useful tool when it comes to conducting annual reviews or making the decision to separate. You cannot defend your decision by stating to your team member or their attorney that they were frequently late for work, violated several of your policies, and were rude to your clients. Statements without dated, clear documentation are pure gold to an attorney claiming unfair dismissal of their client.

> *Justice? You get justice in the next world, in this world you have the law.*
> **—WILLIAM GADDIS**

A good piece of advice to any leader is to create a list of what to include in every team member's file, which of course includes the standard legal requirements and an added list of anything that is pertinent to the position. Be quick to shred the voided check new team members provide when they sign up for direct deposit, but maintain and update emergency contact information for the team. It's not unusual to discover that an emergency contact form completed over ten years is so outdated that the next of kin is now the team member's ex-spouse, the doctor on record has changed, and allergies they previously didn't have listed are now life threatening. Suddenly your good intentions become a liability. I like to refer to this as an "It's All About You" document that contains more than just emergency contacts and allergies. Update it regularly, and also consider finding out what their favorite snack, soda, or candy is. Use that information when there's an opportunity to celebrate something they did well. Leave a note with the snack, soda, or candy, and sit back contently knowing that you connected with your team member in a way that nearly 100 percent of businesses just don't. One piece of advice: Don't ask these questions unless you are committed to delivering on this idea. Otherwise, you're just wasting time.

The "It's All About You" document is particularly useful when a team member leaves you. Within that checklist, you might include items that should be retrieved, such as keys, access codes, laptops, cell phones, or uniforms. A word of caution, though: do not make the mistake of violating the law by making any team member sign a document that requires them to return anything to you before their last paycheck. That is not permitted by law. Don't make it difficult either. It's not worth the reputation you will earn for withholding money that was earned and owed. You can refer to the Department of Labor to understand more about the illegality of withholding checks.

Finally, there's the issue of who has access to a team member's file and when that access is appropriate. Generally speaking, a team member is entitled to see most, if not all, of the contents with reasonable notice to human resources. Know the laws in your state, as each state can be different. For instance, California is strict about what a team member must be able to review. Again, think about what is reasonable and what is not. There is no logical excuse for restricting access to a policy you required a team member to sign. The same goes for time and attendance records, vacation requests, or prior reviews. Also, don't store team member files in an office, filing cabinet, or drawer where others have easy access—this is a big no-no. Even if it's in your office and you don't suspect anyone would pry, it's not worth taking the chance of having to defend yourself in court against a disgruntled team member who claims someone read something in their file.

Hire character. Train skill.

—PETER SCHUTZ

I thoroughly endorse this quote. In today's world, it couldn't be more appropriate.

This HR quote comes from Peter Schutz, the CEO of Porsche between 1981 and 1987, who went on to become a profoundly impactful motivational speaker within the business world.

Teaching someone to have a positive attitude is difficult. If a candidate seems eager and willing to adapt to challenges and learn new skills, they are likely to be a strong hire.

I have been lucky enough to work with a colleague who embodies the nickname "Bubblegum and Sunshine". Her enthusiasm is infectious. If I had been at her interview, she wouldn't have lasted more than about ten minutes before I offered her the job.

CHAPTER 16

SUBSTANCE ABUSE

a·buse

/əˈbyo͞oz/

use (something) to bad effect or for a bad purpose

With new laws and bills passing the Senate, this subject gets a chapter all its own.

Human resources laws are constantly changing and under one political party's administration are likely to continue at a faster pace in favor of your team members. That's not a political statement so much as a reasonable prediction. America has the munchies, a drinking problem, and more ... but just how protected are you and your team members at work?

Although organized labor union membership dropped during the Obama administration, the National Labor Relations Board issued more prounion decisions than at any other time in thirty years. In 2021 alone, over a hundred new laws and ordinances would affect a variety of subjects from minimum wages to leaves of absence. Just as the unions see new laws made to protect them, we see an ongoing relaxation of laws pertaining to marijuana. Questions arise about how this affects team members and how I have counseled former clients.

The trends to legalize marijuana are not going to slow down. Some state and local laws have changed already, protecting team members who want to enjoy recreational use when they are off duty.

At the time of writing this book, well over a dozen states and Washington, DC, have laws permitting recreational use, and several, still, are lining up. More states are debating legislation and others have laws ready to go into effect. Congress is not missing the opportunity to consider a change, and that alone makes it clear that marijuana is likely to be a legal substance throughout the US before too long.

I spent decades working in a highly regulated industry that pre-screened team members prior to employment. We were testing urine and sometimes hair, spending thousands of dollars to find out what was—in my opinion—truly little. Applicants who are casual users already know that if they abstain for seventy-two-plus hours, they will likely pass a preemployment drug test. Hair tests, which are more expensive, can detect the presence of marijuana from months prior and are rarely used because of the exorbitant costs. My position is that the only thing you learn from a test is how smart the applicant is. The shrewd user abstained for three days, went home, and rolled themselves a celebratory joint once they passed the test. Random testing? That's a whole different subject that deserves its own chapter.

TIME FOR TEA!

As leaders, we've all made mistakes. No matter how bad it is, we feel entitled to give ourselves another chance. Sometimes several. Don't expect your Team Members to be so forgiving.

Laws continue to be developed, modified, and challenged. Don't try to keep up. As great recipes for confusion, look to California and Colorado. Famous for being liberal enough to allow citizens to light up at home, these states theoretically prohibit employers from acting. However, Colorado's own high court has ruled that lawful use is covered by federal law, which means, of course, the use is illegal. California has ruled those laws don't protect team members who consume cannabis. Confused? Me too.

It's quite simple, really.

Estimates from the Substance Abuse and Mental Health Services Administration (SAMHSA) shared a reportedly staggering number of 19.3 million adult Americans had a substance use disorder, equal to 7.7 percent of our population.[11] For any employer with one hundred or more team members, put that in perspective as you look around. I don't share that to scare you, but the reality is we likely employ and meet people every day in the grocery store, a restaurant, or coffee shop who suffer from addiction.

Substance & Alcohol Abuse in US Adults

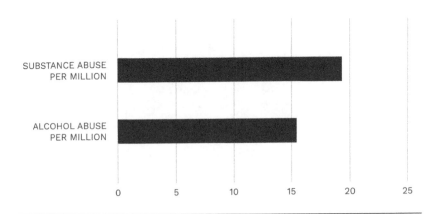

11   "Alcohol, Tobacco, and Other Drugs," SAMHSA, accessed December 1, 2022, https://www.samhsa.gov/find-help/atod.

So what do you do, and how do you protect yourself? Start by thinking about marijuana or any mind-altering substance the way you do about alcohol. A client in Illinois once asked me, "What do I do if one of my team members turns up stoned?" It's simple, really. What would you do if a team member turned up intoxicated?

Your goal is to ensure your team members do the job without being impaired, whether from drugs, alcohol, or both. There's a rule of thumb here I would use: if there's reasonable cause, observed *independently* by more than one person, you can act. Once you have been provided an unbiased viewpoint on whether someone is intoxicated, you must not accuse them of anything other than impairment. Why? Because legally prescribed medications can interact with each other and produce similar results. Tread lightly here.

Be careful to take genuine steps that protect the person you suspect just as much as you are obligated to protect everyone they may interact with. A team member who may have made a life-altering decision should still be treated correctly. Advise them that you would like the contact information of a family member or friend who can come and pick them up. If they are clearly impaired, warn that if they insist on driving home, you won't hesitate to call 911.

Updating your handbook is a must. Better still, compose a new stand-alone "Substance Abuse Policy." Make it broad enough that it covers alcohol, marijuana, opioids, inhalants, and unprescribed drugs of any kind. Finally, use language that can cover anything that could, even remotely, negatively affect any team member's performance. Why? Because although sniffing marker pens, drinking mouthwash, and huffing aerosol vapors is rarer, why not cover yourself? Who knows what's next?

Follow this process up with training. Verbalize your position on important policies. If it's going to save you from a lawsuit—and an eight-hour deposition—it's worth taking thirty minutes to train every team member. Be clear on what *zero tolerance* means.

To any business owners who want to find themselves defending a wrongful termination suit, the process is simple enough. Print up the policy, make enough copies for everyone, and even post one in the break room for good measure. Finally, gather signatures on the policy, file them, and move on. Don't be embarrassed, though, if you still find yourself in court. We will just presume you were high and that's why you ignored this advice!

Verbalize your position on important policies.

CHAPTER 17

LEADERSHIP

---

lead·er·ship

/'lēdər‚SHip/

the action of leading a group of people or an
organization

At the beginning of this book, I touched on one of my favorite subjects as a speaker—*culture*. I'll do the same in my final chapter, except this time on *leadership*.

I can't say definitively if leadership is a talent, a skill, or something you're born with. What I do know is that there are some brilliant leaders out there, and I've been blessed to work with many for whom "brilliant" is an understatement. Some I've worked alongside, and others I've seen in action. Some lead because it's their passion and they want to show others the light. Others do it naturally without realizing just how much impact they have.

Overall, I am committed to the belief that it's a talent that can be taught but not without something inside you that makes you want to be more than just a natural leader. You have to want to be a good and effective one. You must possess the natural abilities to learn from your mistakes, mentally kick yourself and admit when you're wrong, and without any hesitation or thought, help others around you to be good leaders too. Your growth will come from those around you as they follow the paths you have set, and at other times, from the realities of seeing how others lead. Watch for the examples set by still others who expose how you *don't* want to lead. Sadly, there are many good leaders who should be led out the back door, never to be seen again.

TIME FOR TEA!

True leadership requires bravery and as many points of reference as you can find.

To be the leader you want to be, find a leader for yourself who acts as a mentor and, on occasion, your conscience.

Lesson 1: Loyalty is incredibly important when you're a leader. Truthfully, being loyal isn't a talent. It's a human trait you either have or don't. I'm not sure you can be much of a leader without it.

Lesson 2: Called to the carpet by someone I worked with for years, and today call my best friend, prompted what I've chosen as my epitaph and the last line of this book. "My friends told me when I was an idiot or a fool. My enemies told everyone else."

Lesson 3: I learned a lesson simply by inspecting the back of house of one of our restaurants. A timid chef asked me, "Why are you so angry at us when you walk through the kitchens? You never smile, make eye contact, or say hello." The fact that I was on a rushed mission every day to ensure everything was perfect was no excuse, and it couldn't have been more upside down. What I realized and have never forgotten is that the primary focus should have been making sure my crew was happy and had the tools and support they needed to get the job done well. I had the right chef in place, but I was sending the worst message possible. I continued to do my walk-throughs but never again did it without acting like a human being and a leader versus a stuffed shirt inside a suit.

—Head Chef Lula, Mississippi. 2000.

Lesson 4: At the end of a long day, a manager approached me with the decision to separate from a team member. As we talked through her reasoning, it became clear that she had emotional bias. Not unfairly, the manager was frustrated and frazzled, ready to immediately make the call but coming to me in a way that told me she wanted me to take responsibility. A couple of thoughts I shared then still have value today for anyone in a leadership role. First, take the emotion out of the decision—that's a must. Second, sleep on it. Take advantage of a fresh day to see clearly about what your responsibilities are, what your choices are, and which choice is right. I didn't see the leader until about a week later and asked what the outcome had been. Sheepishly, she shared that the team member was still with her department and a candid conversation had satisfied her that additional training and some patience was all they both needed. A win-win situation if ever there was one.

—Tunica, Mississippi. 2002.

Lesson 5: How many times do we come across a team member who passionately believes with every fiber of their being that the next promotion should be theirs? In my earlier days of senior leadership, I attended a meeting where a clear mandate was delivered to the room: "If you want to get promoted, I'll ask you one question before I approve the move. Who replaces you? Who are you developing that can take your place? Without you being able to answer that question, you have failed your duty as a leader and have left this company with a deficit. Someone who is unprepared must fill your position." To me, it was a brilliant move. It shut down the idea that you could and should hold your skills and talents to yourself. At the same time, you could build bench strength for the company.

—Tim Hinkley, Lake Charles. 2003.

Lesson 6: A wonderful man I worked for several years ago asked two brilliant questions that have lived with me ever since. After making any major decision, he would ask: "Okay so now that we've decided to do *X*, how do we *F* it up? Let's pick our plan apart." Frequently that led to us needing to find a different way of getting from point A to point B. Next was the question "Is the pearl worth the dive?" Sometimes we do things based on principal or because we think it's a great solution to what might be a small issue or something lower priority.

—*Michael Frawley, Tunica. 2007.*

Lesson 7: Good leaders don't rush in like fools, but they don't vacillate for weeks or months either. Sometimes we find ourselves a long time into a decision, wishing we had made the tougher decision. And what do we say? "I should have done it months ago, when I knew it was the right thing to do." But we get scared of making an error. To a degree, that's a good thing if your decision is a life-altering one that affects someone else. I was once frustrated by a regional manager who was trying to decide if a team member should leave or stay. Once a week, I'd meet with him and he'd say, "Yup … he's got to go. I'll give you the green light this week." This was invariably followed the next week by: "You know, he's doing better. Hold off." This went on for months. Eventually, I looked at the decision maker and said, "I think I'm going to kill you, Michael! We do this every week. Here's what we're going to do. It's the middle of May. I'll work as hard as I can to get this manager to your standards by the end of August. If by August 31, he hasn't met your expectations, we're done. He goes. If I'm successful and you are happy with him, he stays, and we never talk about this again." He stayed.

—*Michael Frawley, Tunica, Mississippi. 2006.*

Lesson 8: I won't name the person responsible for this memory, but suffice it to say, I share it with everyone I have the privilege of leading. I was working on a project with a very smart man. Ultimately, it was me who was responsible for the outcome, and it wasn't good. After the failure, this man glibly shared his input, saying, "Yeah, I didn't think it would work." I could have killed him. He knew he could have spoken up. Hence one of the little speeches I give everyone new who works with me is "Never hold my hand down the road of ruin. Because if we fail, you're just as much to blame as I am."

—*Vicksburg, Mississippi. 2007.*

Lesson 9: Leadership must recognize that good people can sometimes appear to have changed or lost their way. It's easier to point the finger at their shortcomings and question why they can't adapt to new policies or a different company approach. This was evident when I began to introduce change to a team of over 1,500 team members in 2009. Our assistant general manager shared a profound perspective that has resonated ever since, and one I remember when I see someone who struggles with change. "Sometimes, the company moves ahead, and people get left behind. It's clear that they liked everything just the way it was. It's not their fault, and it's not ours either. But the truth is, we must keep moving or we all get left behind."

—*Will Israel, Kansas City, Missouri. 2010.*

Lesson 10: Learning that you are constantly being watched is tough when your actions are innocent but ill conceived and poorly received. At a town hall meeting with a group of over three hundred team members, I left a few minutes for Q&A at the end of a senior leadership presentation. "Why is it," called out one of our frontline team members, "that when you suits come around, you have cell phones stuck to your ears the whole time?" To the greater amusement of everyone in the room, he added, "Do you stick them on before you leave your offices?" The truth was irrelevant. Our team members didn't care who was on the call, what it was about, or how important it was. The perception was we were rude, and we all know about perception being reality. Avoiding the temptation to feel humiliated or fire back with a snarky remark, I shared how humbled I was by the observation. Much to the annoyance of the executive team, whenever we left our offices—whether alone or not—the use of cell phones was banned.

—*Kansas City, Missouri. 2011.*

Lesson 11: Proudly announcing the financial success of the previous month, our director of finance shared that we had beaten the prior year and our budgeted numbers in both revenues and finance. Everyone was excited and the meeting adjourned quickly as we all headed to lunch to celebrate. The next month, the story could not have been more dire. We had missed every metric in every department. Meetings were called, tough decisions had to be made, and we dived into the numbers until we had a somewhat decent story to share with our corporate leadership team. Before the next set of numbers came out for the following month, I formed an idea I was sure could help leaders remain accountable for short- and long-term results. Thankfully, when the next round of conversations took place, the atmosphere was once again upbeat and congratulatory. Instead of making a quick exit toward the celebratory lunch, I told everyone to enjoy their meal but return to the conference room in exactly an hour. Quizzical looks turned wary as team members wondered whether the numbers were wrong. Everyone was back behind the table in less than thirty minutes.

"What's wrong?" they asked.

"Nothing," I replied. "But when we fell short, we spent hours determining how we missed our numbers and failed to meet expectations, swearing never to make the same mistakes. Yet now that we hit the mark, we spent no time at all figuring out what we did right and how to repeat the same formulas for success." Leadership means having a team that has a real understanding of their wins and their losses.

—*Kansas City, Missouri. 2012.*

> *Successful leaders resist the urge to pause and admire problems when they surface. Unnecessarily sharing the controversial details of a new problem is a form of corporate gossip, particularly when the intention to develop a solution is absent.*
>
> *A leader's superpowers include strategic processing and a persistent dedication to a company's vision. They share in the success with their team, rather than taking credit when things go right and downplaying or deflecting when they don't.*
>
> **—DR. ALEX CULP, DMD, MS**

Lesson 12: A simple lesson in ensuring that you don't fall foul is "Do as I say, not as I do."

"When you get irritated if anyone is late for your meetings," I was told by a vice president of operations who worked for me, "you have to understand how your team feels when you show up late." She added, "We are all busy, and you more than most of us, but we're late for a reason, and probably for the same reasons you are." I was never, or almost never, late again. More importantly, I show respect for anyone who is late for one of my meetings and assume positive intent.

—*Kim Sumimoto, Kansas City. 2013.*

Lesson 13: I spent some time consulting for someone I call a best friend. It was a great ride while it lasted and included several trips in the Caribbean. Even as a consultant, I was given the latitude to act on her behalf, and she frequently introduced me as a corporate executive. I stayed for a week at one location to help her wrangle a team of managers who spent more time arguing and one-upping one another than getting the job done. It was remarkable to me that we were paying these adults to be managers who, quite frankly, needed their heads knocked together. With her typical sense of lighthearted humor, she sent me in to figure it out. I sat there, listening to the back-and-forth bickering. Both sides had valid points, but it was clear that nobody was going to win. That meeting taught me a lesson I have never forgotten and have leveraged ever since. Calling for a time out, I asked everyone to simply stop talking.

"You're both right, and yet you're both wrong," I told them. "But you've left someone out of the argument that deserves a voice and, more importantly, deserves to win your support." They looked around the room as if to find whom I was referring to. "The only one who must win the day is the company. It's not about which of you is triumphant. When you put the company first and do what's right, you're all winners. Your jobs are to figure out what the *right* decision is." After giving them some additional ground rules, I left the room and returned less than an hour later. Decision made. Harmony established. Company won.

—*Aruba. 2015.*

Lesson 14: As a keynote speaker at a Burleson Seminar, I was struck by an extremely humble doctor who was struggling to justify the expectations he had for his team and understand why they wouldn't respond to his leadership. The more I listened, the more I realized that it wasn't him that was at fault. I shared an observation that I have repeated several times since, and it applies to us all: As business owners and leaders, we can't forget we're human. We're entitled to our own minor quirks. We are who we are, and if we don't try to be someone we're not, nobody can think of us as fake or disingenuous. You need to be you. As leaders, we can't expect to unreasonably bend to the will of those we lead. That's the definition of the tail wagging the dog.

Don't take this piece of advice too far!

—Dr. Dustin Burleson DDS, "Burleson Workshop." Vail, Colorado. 2018.

> *What you do has far greater impact than what you say.*
> **—STEPHEN COVEY**

Stephen Covey says you must be extremely self-aware, mature, and principled to be an effective leader. His outlook on leadership is that it takes a certain kind of person to be a leader. Follow him for more great advice!

CONCLUSION

As you think about putting this book somewhere, STOP! The most value comes from having it close at hand where you can use it to refresh your determination to be a human who leads humans. Bookmark your favorite pages or chapters, and make note of or earmark each "Time for Tea" that motivates you to be your best.

What you need to retain is the key elements of leadership that will make you stronger. Never forget that, like me, you will make errors, blunders, and the occasional serious faux pas. That's what makes you human! Just own it, learn from it, and try not to make the same error again.

Great leadership comes neither cheap nor easy. It's the journey you take before looking back and realizing that morale is up and resignations are down. Gauge your successes by measuring how your team communicates with you, supports your decisions, and gives you honest feedback—and whether team members generally seem happy.

I'm including some highlights below that you should cling on to and think about as often as possible to ensure you are on the right track.

TEN CRITICAL STEPS TO SUCCESS

1. A 100 percent commitment will result in success. Do it for your team; do it for yourself.

2. You're a human being. Act like one. Don't be frightened to admit when you're wrong.

3. Culture is the key to success. You have to create it and commit to it.

4. Communication goes both ways. Listen. Learn. Think. Speak.

5. What you want from others is what others want from you.

6. Natural raw talent and a learned education have different value. Respect both.

7. Core values are the ultimate guide of what to do in any situation.

8. The more you put into the review, the more you get out.

9. Handbooks must reflect the human side of you and your company.

10. Appreciate that human beings simply don't like change.

TIME FOR TEA!

A leader without a genuine passion for what they do is like a balloon without helium. Neither reaches their true potential nor is able to reach new heights.

Thank you for reading this book. Use it to become the leader you have the skills, passion, and desire to be. Enjoy the benefits of *Intentional Retention*.

"My friends told me when I was an idiot or a fool. My enemies told everyone else."

ABOUT THE AUTHOR

Sean Barnard has influenced the direction of several companies with annual revenues up to $250 million and the careers of thousands. He is a Society of Human Resources Management Certified Professional and Kolbe Certified Consultant. With forty years of experience working in Europe, the Caribbean, and the United States, he has helped his teams and clients gain the ability to become better leaders who create better workplaces.

Sean started his career as a dealer of roulette in England in 1979 and moved into junior management before making the decision to follow in the footsteps of so many in the casino industry who did not make a lot of money in England. In 1984, he moved to the Bahamas and started back out as a dealer. By the time he left in 1991, he was the casino administrator, overseeing scheduling, payroll, vacations, and training.

Sean was recruited (as a Brit) to come to the US and open one of the first-ever riverboat casinos in Peoria, Illinois. His former boss from the Bahamas, who recruited him to be the casino administrator, not only offered him a job but, when reminded Sean was not American, also promised to sponsor his immigration. Sean took a leap of faith and in 1999 received citizenship. His casino career lasted forty years, including positions as a dealer, administrator, marketer, general manager, senior VP, and consultant. He has owned his own marketing agency and HR consultancy and currently owns a chain of beauty salons.

In 2016, Sean met famous speaker and orthodontist Dustin Burleson, who convinced him that he would be an asset to his seminar and consultancy members in human resources. Being driven and motivated, Sean ran with it, and in 2017 he was introduced to over one hundred orthodontists with his first public speaking engagement for Dustin. Along the way, he picked up a few consultancy jobs while continuing to run the salons (he does not cut hair!). A couple of orthodontists, a firm of accountants, and several beauty shops later, he was up and running. Dustin is Sean's mentor, best friend, and was best man at his wedding to Jason in 2018.

In 2021, the owners of a privately held orthodontics group hired Sean as a consultant and had him complete a "Culture Health Check" of their business. By interviewing over 90 percent of their team members, he was able to diagnose their strengths, opportunities, raw talent, and negative influencers. The owners were committed to fast tracking exponential growth. Doubling size within weeks and blending five companies into one was just the beginning of their plans. Two months later, founder and CEO Dr. Samuel "Jack" Burrow, called and offered Sean the opportunity of chief operating officer. Negotiations over breakfast led to a handshake and a for-sale sign outside of the house he had just purchased in Kansas City, Missouri.

Sean has defined a refreshingly new approach that cuts through the noise of everything HR and demonstrates how you should be leading and retaining a skilled team. He possesses a unique and proven leadership style that gets right to the point, sometimes bluntly, while creating sustainable solutions.